HOW TO USE YOUR
IMAGINATION
TO MAKE MONEY

HOW TO USE YOUR
IMAGINATION
TO MAKE MONEY

James D. Woolf

&

Charles B. Roth

Coachwhip Publications
Landisville, Pennsylvania

How to Use Your Imagination to Make Money,
  by James D. Woolf and Charles B. Roth
First published 1948.
© 2011 Coachwhip Publications

CoachwhipBooks.com

ISBN 1-61646-066-0
ISBN-13 978-1-61646-066-2

CONTENTS

Twenty years ago two young men opened up clothing stores on the same street. Of the same age and graduates of the same school, both men had pleasing personalities, good home training and enough retail sales experience to justify their ventures. Moreover, both were honest, thrifty and industrious.

Today one of these men owns a highly successful department store; the other is struggling to make ends meet in the little shop where he started business.

The main difference between the two men has been a difference in *imagination*.

The book you are about to read is an informative discussion of the nature and use of imagination in business: Imagination is the only capital that every man possesses, active or latent; it is the only all-purpose regenerator of static situations. Imagination makes dull jobs exciting, impossible tasks possible. It transforms a rowboat into a sailboat.

"Where there is an open mind there will always be a frontier," says Charles F. Kettering. You face your competitors, your fellow workers and your community on a threshold of your own making— the frontier of imagination. How freely and how wisely you use your imagination may be the difference between success and failure.

It takes imagination to perceive imagination at work. Opening this book was an indication of imagination on your part. As you read it, let the authors—out of their experience and observations—

help you to make the most of your own endowments of that magical quality.

MERLE CROWELL

1
Open Your Eyes to the Morning Sun

Suppose you were in this predicament: You are sixty-four years old. You have just lost your job. There is a depression on, and men of your age can't find work at anything. You are next door to being broke: your entire resources consist of a hundred dollars cash, plus a tent and a few other items of camping equipment.

If you were in that predicament, just what would you do?

That's exactly what one man I (Roth) know faced in 1934.

George Livingston Baker is this man's name. During World War I he had served as a Captain of Engineers, and after the war he returned to the State Highway Department of his home state, set, he thought, in a lifetime job. But he hadn't reckoned with the depression. There he was, facing a dark, bleak, unenviable future.

Perhaps I should say that the future would have been dark, bleak, unenviable to a man without imagination, but Captain Baker had imagination. And to a man with imagination there is always plenty of hope. This man did as fine and as courageous and as imaginative a thing as I have ever known anyone to do.

He not only found a new career for himself, with the aid of his imagination, but he has been happier, busier, more satisfied with his lot in life since 1934 than he ever was before. In short, he found himself as well as a career.

I want to tell you Baker's story, because it shows definitely that there never is a time when a person with imagination need despair about earning a living or doing the things in life he wants to do.

The thing which Captain Baker did when this cruelest of blows fell on his shoulders was to take his camping outfit, lease a small

tract of land from the Forest Service in the mountains forty miles
from town, and set up his tent. He had an idea. His idea was that a
man could turn pioneer for profit and gain a satisfactory liveli-
hood while doing exactly the things he wants to do.

With his own hands he built a two-room cabin to live in. He
laid in his winter's supply of groceries. By that time his slim capital was about exhausted. Then he turned his imagination to the
task of earning a living.

You would think, wouldn't you, that a man isolated from society, living atop a mountain, would have to have an outside income
to exist at all. But you don't know what kind of imagination this
man Baker has. He opened both eyes to the morning sun—and all
around him he saw opportunities other men missed for making
himself useful, for earning a good living.

Six years later, when he left that mountain retreat (for the same
reason that Henry David Thoreau left Walden Pond—because "he
had other lives to live"), Captain Baker had several thousand dollars and the richest kind of memories of half a dozen years lived in
exactly the way he had always wanted to live.

You may be wondering just how he did it. The answer: he did it
by applying his imagination to the practical, everyday problem of
earning a living.

"I had been used to regular pay checks all my life," this doughty
old warrior explained to me, "and knew little about earning a living
in any other way. But I figured there would always be a demand
for someone if he could point out needs. So I started asking myself
how I could be useful to someone up there in the mountains.

"It was amazing the answers that came in response to my turning imagination loose on that problem. Instead of worrying about
keeping myself busy and earning enough money for groceries and
tobacco, I was actually so busy within a month's time I was turning people away.

"And I really had to stop having ideas, because I was afraid if I
had too many I'd try to do too many things and so wouldn't have
the leisure which I had gone to the mountains to enjoy."

But exactly what did he do—what specific ways did he find to
earn money?

"During the six years I lived on that mountain," is the reply, "I followed all told thirty-six different vocations—found thirty-six different ways that I could earn money, even though I was far from the places where men live.

"It would take a good deal of time for me to describe all thirty-six of these ideas, but let me give you a few examples of how I turned my imagination into money.

"One of the first things I discovered when I went up there was that a good many tourists from the East are afraid to drive on mountain roads. An experienced mountain driver myself, I offered to drive their cars. They could enjoy the scenery better anyway if somebody else did the driving. At a dollar an hour they considered this a great bargain.

"That idea led to another. Why not act as a guide to fishermen and hunters? I charged $50 a week for guiding parties through the mountains. That made both of us happy.

"I noticed that my mountain neighbors didn't go to the bother to have a garden. I planted one. There were no marketing problems in the fall when my garden stuff was ready—it was easy money.

"During my first winter I made myself some rustic furniture out of the pine trees on my place. When visitors admired it, offered to buy it, that gave me another idea—make furniture. Every winter I spent my spare time at this job. The proceeds from my furniture sales were enough to keep me all during the year, even if I had no other sources of income.

"But I had many other sources. I concocted a cold remedy from mountain herbs, for instance, and had a hard time keeping it in stock. Another plant I discovered acted in killing the craving for tobacco. I had orders for that from a dozen states. I tanned the hides of the game animals my sportsmen had killed during the season when I was guiding them, and mounted the heads. And I picked up $2 a week by acting as correspondent for the county seat paper.

"I say that it doesn't make any difference where you are; if you can use your imagination, you can always earn a living. I proved that to my satisfaction."

This story of George Livingston Baker, however, has an interesting sequel to bring it up to date. After he left the mountains, he spent time in various places, but eventually drifted back to his home state of Colorado An old man now, past his mid-seventies, he could have retired and taken his ease. Did he do it? His imagination wouldn't let him—there were too many interesting things to do to retire.

Just last week I had a letter from him, as fine and as courageous a letter as I ever saw.

"You may be surprised to learn," he began, "that I am embarking on an entirely new career—one that I think I will like ever so much. Believe me or not, I am now a water colorist! What's more, I sell what I paint—which makes me a professional artist.

"I didn't know till last March that I could sketch in pencil and do water colors. But I started experimenting and found I did such a creditable job folks were willing to pay money for my pictures. I started drawing sketches and selling them for thirty-five cents, but I get three dollars for everything I do now—and I can't keep up with the demand."

When I asked you in opening this chapter what you would do if you were in Mr. Baker's position, you probably had no answer ready. Now you know what one man did. It seems to me that anyone, by the use of a little imagination, could do just as well—provided he were willing to open his eyes to the opportunities all around him.

Sometimes these opportunities are not the obvious, patent things. Often they are by-products of other ideas.

Let me give you an example of what I mean. One of the sensational postwar products today is known as Rex-Air, a vacuum cleaner manufactured in Detroit. Proclaiming advantages over all other vacuum cleaners, this product is sweeping the country. The fascinating thing about Rex-Air is that it didn't start out as a vacuum cleaner at all. It is one of those by-product ideas I am telling you about—a by-product idea that has become a multimillion-dollar business!

This is the story. For a number of years before he passed away Fred Fisher, the elder of the Fisher brothers who manufacture automobile bodies, suffered from asthma. In his home in Detroit, Mr.

Fisher had air conditioning to wash the air and hence make his life tolerable. But traveling for him was a penance.

He and his associates devised a portable air-conditioning unit that could be carried in the car or on the train and set up in a hotel room. It worked perfectly. They had no thought of turning it into a commercial product until one of Mr. Fisher's associates discovered that this air conditioner not only washed the air but also removed the dust from the floor. Why, he asked himself, his imagination rushing ahead, why not offer it as a vacuum cleaner? Millions of American homes would buy it.

This proved to be a practical idea, and thus was the Rex-Air business born—somebody, you see, had "opened his eyes to the morning sun."

Let me tell you about another man who found a rich and satisfying career because he was willing to let his imagination go. Arthur Pohndorf was his name.

A mining man interested in rocks and minerals of all kinds because they were his stock in trade, Mr. Pohndorf was wont to take a busman's holiday every summer in Arizona, visiting the petrified forests and becoming thrilled by the grotesque and beautiful shades and colorings of prehistoric trees turned to stone. Everybody in Arizona knew about petrified wood. To most Arizonians they were just uninteresting lumps of stone cluttering up the landscape.

But to Arthur Pohndorf they were something more, something much more. They were beautiful gem stones which women could wear proudly and cherish and hand down from generation to generation. That is what Arthur Pohndorf saw when he looked over the desolate wastelands covered by chunks of petrified wood.

When his mining business failed, he moved to the city and opened a small mineral shop, selling mineral specimens to collectors. But in the back of his mind was his dream—jewelry from petrified wood.

He went to Arizona, and brought back some of the better specimens. These he sent to Europe for polishing. Expectantly he awaited the first shipment of polished pieces of his beloved wood— and was ecstatic when he beheld them. He had never dreamed of the gradations of coloring, the mysterious hues, the fascinating, intricate designs. He was seeing what no one had ever seen before—the possibilities for a business where others had found only a passing interest.

Into various forms of jewelry he had petrified wood made, into rings and pendants and necklaces and tie pins, in addition to objects such as ash trays and book ends and desk stands.

When he offered these to the American public, he found as much enthusiasm for the new jewelry as he himself had for it. Petrified wood became the rage. It is still one of the most popular sellers, now a standard jewelry item, because Arthur Pohndorf was willing to use his imagination.

You see, it doesn't make any difference where you are; if you will open your eyes and let your imagination have full sway, you will find some way to capitalize on conditions around you.

I know a mail-order man, for instance, who had to go to Florida one winter because the climate in his home town of Chicago was too rigorous for him. He was convalescing from an attack of pneumonia; his expensive illness left him with very little money. When he got to Florida he too opened his eyes to the morning sun. He saw the possibility of selling Florida oranges by mail. So he rented a mailing list of a thousand names, wrote a simple letter and modest circular, and sent them out. Back came a sufficient number of orders to encourage him in going ahead. He did. This was the establishment of a satisfactory half-year business. For fifteen years this man has been blissfully engaged during the winter months with his Florida mail-order business; during the rest of the year with his big-city business in Chicago.

Here's another—Billy B. Van, the old-time vaudevillian. He found his big adventure in imagination in Vermont. Here he had gone to recover from tuberculosis. The scent of the pine trees enchanted Billy B. Van. He believed, besides, they contributed something to his recovery, and he was grateful. How could he share this delightful pine odor with others?

For a man of his lively imagination it didn't take long to find the answer—pine-tree soap. He organized a small local company, and began selling his pine-tree soap. The company grew to large size. It is still going strong, this imagination-born soap business.

While I'm telling you about what imagination will do in helping you make money, let me take a few lines to tell you what it can do to help you live longer. It is a fact that men engaged in work requiring imagination have longer life on the average than men whose jobs do not require this mind force. Poets, for instance, have an average life of sixty-six years; novelists, sixty-seven; historians, seventy-three; philosophers, sixty-five; inventors, seventy-two.

Individual members of all these groups live far beyond the average span, and seem to me to live more eagerly, actively, and exuberantly than other persons live. Take Tolstoy, who is mentioned in a later chapter. He lived to be eighty-four. Goethe lived to be eighty-three and completed his masterpiece *Faust* just a year before his death. Victor Hugo lived to be eighty-three; Ibsen, seventy-eight; Titian, ninety-eight, and Michelangelo, eighty-nine.

From what I have told you thus far in the chapter you could correctly conclude that the rewards of imagination, provided you are willing to open your eyes, are invariably good, and that there is no bar of age, or location, or condition, or time that can prevent you from attaining more from your life.

Suppose I give you a few suggestions for opening your eyes to what goes on around you every day.

The first thing for you to do is to *analyze your day's work to see if there's anything you are overlooking, any new ideas you could put into your life.*

It's a funny thing about human beings, but we all fail to see the forest for the trees. We go far afield for ideas while all the time our best ideas are all around us. Most new inventions, as a matter of fact, are made by men who are not engaged in the field in which the invention is made. Why couldn't the insiders see what the outsiders saw? They were looking too far afield, instead of close to home.

Suppose you start turning over stones close to home, seeking for ideas that are close to where you sit. They are the best ideas you can have, the easiest to put into use, the surest ideas in your life.

One of my friends has been markedly successful in introducing new ideas, new methods into his business. If he overlooks any bets,

I don't know what they are, because he's always about a mile and a half ahead of everyone else in his industry.

I asked him how he did it, how he found the time to carry on this quest for new ideas while managing the affairs of an intricate business.

He told me about his practice, and it is one I should like to recommend for you. His practice is to set aside fifteen minutes each evening for his imagination period.

For years he has done this. Nine-tenths of the ideas that he has used in gaining the top position in his field have come during these imagination periods, he told me the other night.

During this fifteen-minute period he merely sits alone and thinks, preferably in a darkened room so as to have no distractions of any kind. He lets his imagination roam over as wide a territory as it chooses for its peregrinations. He asks himself if he's overlooking any bets. If so, what are they? Is there anything new he should be introducing into his business but isn't?

My friend is in a highly competitive business; I have heard his competitors complain but I have never heard him complain. He apparently is always just a jump or two ahead of anybody in the same field.

Try this same plan for a while. I believe I can predict that after two or three weeks of getting your imagination used to the freedom you will be granting it, you will be flooded by ideas—have more ideas than you thought yourself capable of having.

Now for my second suggestion: *Let your imagination have free rein—operate absolutely without inhibitions.*

Among the men whose imagination I admire most there is one who springs ideas on me occasionally that he and I both know are off the beam. In fact, one of his favorite expressions, in introducing me to a new idea, is, "Now, you're going to think I am completely crazy. And I may be. But it seems to me that this idea might work."

Then he gives me his latest idea. Sometimes it's a good idea. Often it isn't. But that doesn't matter too much, for he and I both realize that if you want your stream of imagination to flow unimpeded, you had better not restrict it—just let it have free flow.

I asked him the other day what percentage of ideas of his were good ideas—ideas on which he was able to build. He thought for a while and said:

"Oh, if one in ten is good I think I am doing pretty well. If I hit two in ten, I am elated. Suppose a man hit center only once in fifty times. That man can become a millionaire.

"I'm willing to kill nine ideas outright—if the tenth is one that will work."

Third suggestion: *When you get a good idea, let it set for a few hours or a few days to see whether it seems as good after several days as it appeared in the white heat of creation.*

Your idea may be as good after a day or two—or it may not be. Very often ideas have a way of turning very sour when you take them out after a lapse of a day or two. At best they might appear to you, on second glance, to have certain "bugs" you must work out before the idea is good. See if you can work these bugs out. If you can, fine. If you can't, remember that if you will encourage yourself and your imagination, you will never run out of ideas, for, as one man told me, after I had pointed out flaws in his latest idea that made it impractical, "That's all right. Nothing is lost. Ideas are as thick as the stars in the heavens—if you know how to reach for them. And I know how."

Fourth suggestion: *Review your ideas now and then, bringing them up one at a time, examining them critically, seeing if any of them have reached the stage where you can put them into use.*

Often ideas which are impracticable at one stage of your life become practical a little later. That is what happened not long ago to one of my friends.

Ten years before, he had an idea for a new kind of service business—a cleaning establishment that would operate on a more personal basis than the cleaning places in his city. He thought at the time the idea was sound, but he was engaged in the practice of his profession of accountancy. He didn't want to give that up to open a cleaning business.

Times changed. His health forced him to give up accountancy, and then the idea he had had ten years before beckoned to him. He brought it out into the open once more. Was it sound? Would it still work? What was wrong with it?

With just a little changing around, the idea seemed to be ready for use; so he opened his first unit. He has been extremely successful with an idea he had lived with for a decade before he was ready to put it into effect.

My final suggestion: *Be tough with your ideas.*

It's very simple—also very foolish—to have what is called "pride of authorship" in connection with an idea. The fact is that not all ideas are good and that not all ideas you have can be carried out. It is better for you to be tough and critical of your ideas than to try to carry out every one and let the public be tough and critical with them. And this the public will be, because in the long run an idea has to be sound to win.

Before you go ahead too far on an idea that might not be sound, test it out in a small way. The easiest way to do this is to ask the opinion of others. Don't take their criticism too seriously, and if you believe in the idea, go ahead regardless of contrary advice from friends or others. But get all sides to the question first.

Very often you will overlook some important things, because you are too close to your idea and too much prejudiced in its favor to see the shortcomings. An outside, disinterested point of view would pick out these flaws. It is a good idea to get such an opinion.

But, as I say, don't be swayed too much by it, and if you have profound belief in your idea, go ahead with it as far as you can.

Two youngsters took an idea for a new kind of news magazine to half a dozen different "authorities" a few years ago. Both were enthusiastic over their chances to succeed. But of the six men whose opinion was asked, only one saw any possibility for the new magazine. The others pointed out that there were already too many magazines on the market, and another would fail. One man saw its possibilities, encouraged the budding publishers to go ahead.

They took his advice, ignored the advice of the other five. And it is well that they did, because if Henry Luce and Briton Hadden had listened to the five—had believed them rather than themselves—they never would have made the tremendous success that came to them as publishers of *Time* magazine.

Don't stop having new ideas. Don't stop opening your eyes to the morning sun. Keep looking for ideas everywhere. Keep getting enthusiastic over them. If one isn't feasible and you have to drop it, don't be too much downcast over that. Keep on trying. For there is no adventure in life more exciting or satisfying than the adventure of having ideas. It does something to you nothing else ever will do. Other pleasures may in time become cloying, but having ideas never will.

One of my friends always pleased me with the tremendous kick he got out of living. He was a man of vivid imagination, and I suspected there was a relationship between his imagination and his zest for living. So one day I asked him about it.

He said, "Listen. I open my eyes each day to the morning sun. I look upon each day as a fresh adventure in ideas. Because I look for ideas, I always have something to live for, something new in my life, something exciting. Don't you see how simple it all is?"

I said I did. And I have repeated his formula for your benefit. If you want more out of your life—more in profit, more in the zest for living as well—apply this formula.

2
Imagination—the Miracle Worker

When L. C. Probert, Chesapeake & Ohio vice-president, dreamed up the railroad's beloved cat "Chessie," he performed a notable act of business imagination.

Back in 1935, the road put on a new air-conditioned train, the *George Washington*, of which it was very proud. Its quiet, streamlined sleeping cars were made for Sleep with a capital "S," and now the problem was how to stir up the interest of the public.

The old bromide "Sleep Like a Top," for example, didn't suit Probert at all as a slogan. For days he lashed his imagination—and then, at last, came the idea of Chessie, who "Sleeps like a Kitten" on the C. & O. (together with her old man, Peake, and the two kids). Chessie hit the jackpot. So adored is this fetching cat that her fan mail is now close to a million letters, and more than two million calendars have not kept up with the demand for her portrait. Gifts ranging from cartons of catnip mice to crates of oranges flood in on her.

When Frederick Henry Harvey, founder of the great chain of restaurants and hotels along the storied route of the Santa Fe, dreamed up the celebrated Harvey Girls, he also performed an act of business imagination.

Those demure, well-mannered, churchgoing maidens, primly uniformed in plain black dresses with white "Elsie collars," were the answer to a hankering in the heart of the untamed pioneer of the late eighties. They played a big part in making eating—good eating—a civilized business in the wild and woolly West, and in bringing fame and fortune to the Harvey venture.

Neither enterprise nor thrift nor industry nor determination nor courage nor all these fine qualities combined could have produced these ideas in Probert's and Harvey's minds if imagination had been lacking.

Just what do we mean by imagination? Is it not *synthesis*, the putting of things together, as against *analysis*, the taking of things apart? Is it not the relating of one thought or object to another and different one—the joining of separate ideas or elements into a wholly new concept? Is it not, put another way, the ability, upon observing the good effect of any force in one instance, to construct around that same force its probable good effect in another instance?

Charles E. Duryea saw his wife spraying herself with perfume, an atomizer reducing it to a fine mist; he saw also the need of a device that would "atomize" gasoline into the cylinders of the new automobile engine he was developing. He related those two observations, and presto, his imagination produced the first practical carburetor! The principle for his reaper is said to have come to Cyrus McCormick while he was having his hair cut: he related the action of the barber's clipper to the mechanical cutting of wheat— and there was his idea! Thomas Callahan saw an object of transparent paper (possibly a chewing-gum wrapper) and he noted how easily printing could be read through it; then he saw how much time typists consume addressing envelopes. His imagination joined one observation to the other—and he became the inventor of the popular "window envelope."

But enough of mechanical inventions. Let us look at the workings of imagination—of *seeing* and *relating*—in everyday business transactions. We can scarcely go lower in the business scale than a boy seeking a way to make: money. Edward Bok, one-time great editor of the *Ladies' Home Journal*, desperately needed a job, as a lad, when his mother failed in health. He was looking into the window of a bakery one day after the baker had just arranged his display of fresh goods. The baker said, "Look pretty good, don't they?" Bok replied, "They would if your window was cleaner." "True enough," answered the baker. "I wonder if you will clean it?" In this way young Bok got the job of keeping the baker's window clean for fifty cents a week. Bok used his imagination: he related one attraction to another—a clean, bright window with a tempting exhibit of fresh bakery goods. He conveyed the information, *not merely that he sought work*, but that any baker would want to show his handiwork through sparkling glass.

Consider as another example Percy C. Johnston. Sixteen, his father dead, he ran errands for a bank in Lebanon, Kentucky. Ambitious, he soon realized that old-fashioned hard work alone wasn't enough. If he was to win a more important place, and quickly, he saw he would have to create something of special value to the bank, which is exactly what he did—*with an idea.*

Young Johnston said to the bank's president, "This bank wants to do business with farmers all over the county, yet it seems to know little about them. I don't think it knows which farmers are capable and industrious, which are going downhill, which have good farms and which have poor ones. It's my idea that this bank could do a lot more business—and with less risk, too—if it had such information. I want to go out and get it."

Field surveys in those days were a rarity. Here indeed was a new thing in Kentucky! But it sounded good, and Percy was given the green light.

Hitching his horse to a buggy, off he went—and he didn't return until he had had a friendly visit with every farmer in Marion County. Then he marched into the president's office with a written record of the size and character of every farm, the condition of the buildings, the number of livestock, the kind and quantity of the farm machinery, whether the farmer had a bank account (and, if so, where), whether the farm was mortgaged, and so on.

Such a mass of vital, firsthand data the bank had never dreamed of acquiring. Percy had a new thing the bank wanted, his job was at once secure—and, as it turned out, so was his future. Twenty-three years later Percy C. Johnston—*largely because he continued to use his imagination*—was made president of the great Chemical Bank and Trust Company of New York.

Are you thinking of investing in real estate? Let's see what imagination can do here. Not long ago, a Santa Fe businessman bought a five-room adobe house; a hundred years old, it badly needed repair. Chided by a friend about his six-thousand-dollar purchase, this man replied, "George, you are not using your imagination. I see this house, not as it is, but *as it can be.* I see not that yard enclosed by its slat fence, but a sunlit patio hidden behind a picturesque adobe wall. I see not that plain painted door, but a lovely old hand-carved Spanish one. I see an adobe Indian fireplace added to the living room, and I can almost smell now the fragrance of the crackling piñon logs. A thousand dollars or two for a little dressing up, George, and tenants will be competing to live in the historic and charming 'Century House.' The remodeling is less than half finished, but I've already had three chances to sell it at a fine profit."

Here are two brothers who, in the late 1930's, were going broke with their idle ice-making plant at little Hynes, California. It was a hay and dairy community—and anything but a "play" town—and surely an ice skating rink was the last thing its people would go for.

But Frank and Lawrence Zamboni thought differently. Their "practical" and "realistic" friends tried to discourage them, said that "on the face of it the idea was ridiculous." But the two brothers looked beyond "the face of it," which is what the imaginative thinker always does, and put their last dollars in a beautiful rink. They opened free classes for children, formed skating clubs, arranged shows, contests, pageants, taught sun worshipers that ice is fun, too. But for two long years their big idea was a loser. Then, slowly at first, now faster, soon faster still, the new rink took hold, and success was in sight. Today 6,000 persons weekly come from miles around to skate to the music of Iceland's $45,000 Wurlitzer Pipe Organ, and to witness its spectacular ice shows. Iceland is big business, a dream come true.

Imagination did that; nothing else could have created that idea in the face of "plain facts" that dismayed the hard-headed friends of Frank and Lawrence Zamboni.

The imaginative man considers all the instincts, longings, prejudices, and passions of mankind. It is related of a New York department store that it found itself overstocked with low-priced pianos. The stereotyped advertising appeals failed to get results.

Advertisements that told of the merits of this particular piano, of its sweet tone, its lovely finish, its low price, and so on, got no-where. Then one morning the newspapers came out with a large ad displaying this headline: *Make Your Daughter a Lady*. The text asserted that music was the soul of culture, that ability to play the piano was an important social asset. Here was a real connection with a human yearning—and it was the result not of fancy writing but of an imaginative understanding of what makes people do things. Twenty-four hours later every piano was sold.

What that piano ad sold, in the words of sales expert Elmer Wheeler, was "not the steak but the *sizzle*"; not pianos as such, but the satisfaction of a human want. Hidden in everything you sell are "sizzles." Thus wheat flakes are not merely a cereal but "The Breakfast of Champions." Only in fairly recent years have businessmen fully understood this philosophy of the "sizzle." One of the earliest advertisers to apply it effectively was a maker of toilet soap. The advertising had been emphasizing certain medi-cinal values of the soap, whereas most other brands were sold merely as cleaners. In 1910, the sale of the product, despite its ex-cellent quality, was shrinking badly. The problem was put up to an advertising man, Stanley Resor—and his imagination saved the day. The advertising from then on sold not soap as such, but *"A Skin You Love to Touch."* Demand picked up at once. Today volume is so great that the soap sells for less than half its original price.

Consider what Daniel J. O'Connel did with the humble ham-burger. Purveying it in upstate Illinois in the traditional hurry-up white-tile lunchroom, he had very little edge on his competition. Studying the patrons he *didn't* get, he fell to wondering why it was necessary to serve this great American favorite in such common-place surroundings. Risking his capital, he went to Chicago and opened one small beautifully done establishment, its paneling solid walnut, its lighting fixtures authentic antiques, its walls hung with fine old prints. Hamburger restaurateurs were appalled at such folly. Never had the lowly hamburger been enjoyed amid such el-egance—and the public loved it. Now O'Connel has six such places, each a little gem of interior decorating and each featuring ham-burgers, apple pie, and coffee as its main culinary attractions. From a hundred or so meals a day ten years ago O'Connel now serves 12,000 low-priced meals a week, with yearly sales well over one million dollars. It took nerve for O'Connel to shatter tradition and invade the fiercely competitive Chicago market, but it was his imagination that gave him both his idea and the confidence to carry it out.

If you were marketing a toothbrush and wanted increased demand for it, what would you do? Assuming that your brush was as good as it could be made, by what act of imagination could you cause it to stand out competitively? That was the problem that faced John T. Woodside, president of the Weco Company, in 1930.

Most toothbrushes were then anything but clean: they were displayed "nude" in open baskets, and customers would soil them by thumbing the bristles. Woodside decided to sterilize his brushes and keep them clean in sealed glass containers—believe it or not, a brand-new notion fifteen years ago. He now had an inviting, fresh-looking product, one that the public took to so readily that sales have quadrupled since the revolutionary introduction of the sparkling glass bottle. Many things have contributed to its success, of course, but none so much as this single act of one man's imagination. Such is the stuff that all merchandising ideas are made of: little plus-values that often mean the difference between mediocrity and leadership. How simple they seem—*after the event!*

Another single act of imagination—a very simple idea—turned a small Detroit jewelry firm into a large company of national repute.

It was again a clear case of relating one thing to another. For a long time Ernest E. and Carl O. Bross, the company's president and vice-president, respectively, had felt that there might be a countrywide market for a decorated wedding ring to take the place of the customary cold and unadorned band. But the Bross brothers had only *half* an idea; the other half—how to decorate this new ring?

Then came the other half of the idea, and once thought of, it was astonishingly simple. Was not the orange blossom the traditional wedding flower? "Why," asked Ernest of Carl, "didn't we think of it years ago?"

Many designs were made. The problem of putting a suitable design on a narrow band was not easy. And almost everybody insisted the old plain band was best. But finally even the prejudice of the clergy was overcome by a beautiful design of orange blossoms chased on a band of gold or platinum.

Through the years since then there have been changing styles. Diamonds have become more generally used for decorative purposes. Today there are a variety of designs numbering in the hundreds. But it was the orange blossom flower which changed it all—an idea so obvious nobody thought of it before. Today leading jewelers everywhere sell "Orange Blossom Wedding Rings by Traub."

Perhaps there is no greater challenge in business than the selection of a trade name. Often the appeal of the name is a primary force in attracting customers. The quality of imagination in the naming of a great many products and services is appallingly second-rate. Nobody has ever made a count, but there must be thousands of public eating houses known by such names as Brown's Restaurant, Rochester Restaurant, Main Street Café, Harry's Café, Joe's place, and—worst of all!—just plain Eats.

The originators of the following names—and how delightful it is occasionally to come upon them in one's travels—had imagination: The Farm Cupboard, The Pump Room, The Little Traveler's Tea Room, The Old Mill Dam Tavern, Johnny Cake Inn, The Camellia House, The Robin Hood, and The Spinning Wheel Tea Room. Rare indeed are such suggestive names as Beauty-rest (for a mattress), Land O'Lakes (for a butter), Log Cabin and Brer Rabbit (for a sirup and a molasses), Big Ben (for a clock), and Minute Man (for a fire extinguisher). Chase & Sanborn Tea was changed in name to Tender Leaf Brand Tea, and sales have ever since been going up. The United States Gutta Percha Paint Company tried several trade names, hit on Barreled Sunlight, now consider it a priceless sales asset. Dale Carnegie says the success of his famous best seller was in large part due to its name, *How to Win Friends and Influence People*. It took him eighteen months to think it up.

When seeking to change a fundamentally bad business situation into a good one, we must beware of the mere invention of "stunts," a very different thing from the kind of imagination we have been talking about.

No mere "invention," no catchy advertising slogan, would have solved the problem of Western Union back in 1900. Business was bad, the service not widely used: short telegrams were inadequate and unsatisfactory; long telegrams were too expensive. That was Fact Number One. Fact Number Two was the costly necessity of maintaining a twenty-four hour staff even though business offices were closed at night and people at home in bed. Mostly the night staff sat idle. Then along came a man of powerful imagination, Theodore N. Vail, once a station agent, who saw the relationship of those two facts—a relationship nobody in the organization had seen before. Nobody, in fact, had ever been aware of any trouble. The ideas Vail created—the Night Letter, the Day Letter, the Week-end Cable, etc.—are often described as inventions. They were not inventions at all: they were the end result of Vail's imaginative insight into underlying causes, and they became institutions of great service to the public and of profit to the company.

Twenty years ago the publisher who tried to sell a new book by mail usually ended up in the hole. A mail-order business to be profitable must permit a reasonable margin for cost of selling—and the margin simply was not there in the single sale of a two- or three-dollar book. If the advertising cost could only be applied against several new books instead of one, the thing would be easy. But how? Publishers were stumped; the problem awaited a man of imagination.

That man was Harry Scherman, a New York advertising expert. The public, he realized, bought the new books haphazardly, spasmodically, often unwisely. "Why shouldn't people," he wondered, "subscribe to new books just as they do to their favorite monthly magazines?" That was it! He had it—the now renowned Book-of-the-Month Club, its titles selected by an authoritative Editorial Board, and its basic selling appeal, which has never changed, "Don't miss the important new books you want to read."

Note that Harry Scherman didn't invent "stunts," such as premiums, to stimulate one-time book sales. His idea was fundamental and sound, for both publishers and readers it supplied a real need, and in testimony of this is a customer list of more than 800,000 families.

Ten or twelve years ago scared wives demanded of thousands of air-minded husbands that they stay off planes. Here was a problem for an imaginative thinker, a label that precisely fits United Air Lines' William A. Patterson. Knowing how dearly women love a bargain, Patterson offered to take along every wife—free!—with her husband, no matter how long the air journey. Women, their timidity forgotten, grabbed at this irresistible bargain—thousands of them. Other important air lines followed suit, and within a few months air travel reached a new high. Patterson's idea was not a stunt; it was an ingenious attack on a basic problem. It was Patterson also who, in 1930, pioneered the world's first air stewardesses, 2,000 of whom today ride the skyways. Now Patterson's imagination is again pioneering: this time it's the de luxe planes operated for mothers and babies, and equipped with bassinettes, hot and cold milk and such stuff for formula feeding, disposable diapers, baby kits, toys, and infant what-nots of every description.

Only the idea that is of genuine service has any lasting business value—which brings up the achievement of James L. Kraft. In 1913, Kraft, twenty-nine and out of a job—and dogged with business misfortune for thirteen years—began peddling cheese door to door.

The cheese then sold wasn't much to brag about. It wasn't always too clean, and the quality was so up-and-down that the housewife seldom got the same flavor twice in a row. Some halfhearted attempts at packaging had been made, with no luck: warm weather made bacteria grow, the cheese swelled, and then the packages and jars blew up. Enough to discourage any man.

Now let's see what a little of that imagination we have been considering did for peddler Kraft. And let's see, too, how *synthesis*—the putting of things together—gave the world a packaged cheese of standardized quality and flavor.

As Kraft rattled his little cheese wagon around Chicago's streets, he noticed that milk bottles, sun-warmed on family doorsteps, *didn't* blow up. Kraft figured that out easily enough: pasteurization prevented bacteria growth. At once he began experimenting, and finally, in 1913, he had what he wanted—a sure-fire way to pasteurize cheese, package it so it would keep, and keep in the precise flavors his customers liked best. That idea helped make America a nation of cheese eaters, and today we consume twice as much as we used to.

Nothing that has been said so far implies that there is not a proper place in business for "circus." Showmanship often works wonders (see Chapter Twelve). If the product is right, the business sound, novel publicity ideas often work wonders. Swift & Company once promoted a butter substitute by exhibiting on State Street in Chicago the "largest cake in the world." A hundred and five thousand people climbed four flights of stairs to see the room-high wonder, and a cordon of police surrounded the store to keep another hundred thousand out. Overnight, thousands of users were gained, a sales result normally to be expected only after a period of weeks or months of publicity. George Hormel startled the advertising world when, introducing a new soup, he offered "double your money back" to any purchaser not delighted. W. A. Shaeffer, the first to offer a guaranteed *lifetime* fountain pen, had a startler, too. The first "1-cent sale" (two of an item for the price of one plus a cent) gave an imaginative new twist to the bargain offer and jarred many a sleepy merchant.

Crowds blocked traffic in front of a Fifth Avenue store to see Salvador Dali's fur-lined bathtub. Cooper's photographs of men models in transparent cellophane clothes to show their Jockey underwear attracted wide attention. The Sherman Hotel in Chicago has its steam tables on what looks like a toy railroad train, and McCreery's Big Top restaurant looks like a circus tent. Newspapers in and around Burbank, California, give continuous publicity to Neal Parker's "Home Town Register." Hundreds of lonely out-of-towners come into his dry-cleaning establishment to write their names in the Register's forty-eight "State Books," and to look for friends. Ideas like these, eagerly sought, are justified and serve a good business purpose when the products they promote have merit, and business pays well for them.

So far in this chapter examples of the power of imagination in business have been described only briefly. Let us now take a business, a spectacularly successful one, and observe in considerable

detail the reason for its amazing growth. Conrad N. Hilton is un-
questionably the most successful hotel man in America. Let us take
a look at the workings of his mind—at the reach and depth of an
imagination that has spread a string of Hilton hotels across
America from coast to coast which is host to more people than any
other group of hostelries on earth.

Every day 12,000 Hilton guests sleep under a Hilton roof, 3,600
in Chicago at the Stevens alone, far and away the world's biggest.
Every day more than 40,000 guests are fed at Hilton tables. And
twice monthly 10,000 employees draw a Hilton pay check.

The Hilton hotel empire is colossal: there is the swank Town
House on Wilshire Boulevard in Los Angeles, the Loop's famed
Palmer House, and the gigantic Stevens on Michigan Avenue in
Chicago. There are five bustling Hilton hotels in Texas, one in Albu-
querque, New Mexico, one in Long Beach, California, and the Day-
ton Biltmore in Ohio. In New York there are the stately Plaza and
the popular Roosevelt, and just to give the job a bit more gusto,
there is the Palacio Hilton in Chihuahua, in old Mexico.

The amazing thing is that it has all been done in twenty-six
years. Conrad N. Hilton, the man who did it, had his first "hotel"
experience as a boy of sixteen in little San Antonio, New Mexico
(population 760), when he fixed up five rooms over his father's
general store, took in guests, earned and saved enough profits to
put himself through college. Then, enlisting, he fought in World
War I, came back a lieutenant, got in the hotel business in earnest
by buying his first hotel in oil-boomed Cisco, Texas. That was in
1919. Today a seventy-million-dollar hotel property, of which
Conrad Hilton is head man and principal owner, ranks him un-
questionably the Number One man in the United States hotel business.

How did he do it, this boy from a backward New Mexican village? What quality of mind and character does he have that has
made him so successful? What, in short, makes him "tick"? Countless people have asked that question—just as they have always
asked it about every man or woman of outstanding achievement.

The answer can be summed up in one word—*imagination*. Conrad Hilton has a powerful lot of it, and from it came his idea, which

you shall hear about presently; his vision of how far this idea would take him; and the courage he has displayed in seeing it through.

At the very outset of his hotel career, Hilton sensed that the age of leisure, of hotel management by the "servant-proprietor," was over. Ye olden days of "mine host" were fading fast. America was speeding up, and he saw long before most hotel men that techniques in hotel-keeping were not keeping pace. Few hotels were making money, and about 85 per cent of them went to the wall during the hard years following World War I.

Conrad Hilton—and here you see imagination at work—has always been able to see things with the other fellow's eyes. He is unfailingly objective in his viewpoint. Thinking of himself as a hotel guest—not as a hotel owner—he studies his patrons with vast curiosity, sees them as fast-stepping, go-getting, impatient Americans with no time for the leisurely inefficiency of the oldtime innkeeper. What sort of hotel service does modern America want, he asks himself day in and day out, *and what will it want in the future?*

What they want above all else, he is convinced, is efficiency—modern, streamlined efficiency on just four counts: comfort, speed, courtesy, cleanliness. *Business efficiency.*

Out of this conviction comes Hilton's philosophy of hotel-keeping. Here it is, the big idea that is building his empire: The only hotel that can be a really good hotel—good in the quality of those four things guests want—is the *hotel that operates at a profit.*

Conrad Hilton has been referred to as a "balance sheet operator," and he truly is that. He determinedly runs his hotels to make money, not only because he likes to make money for himself and his shareholders and his employees but also because he knows there is no other way to give his guests fine hotel service. The badly run hotel that is constantly on the border line of bankruptcy must of necessity cut corners and give penny-pinching service to its guests.

Hence it is that Hilton's first consideration is caliber of business management when he adds another hotel to his string. The man he installs to run it need not be a connoisseur of rare wines, but he *must* be a connoisseur of business statistics. Hilton is said to be the first hotel man anywhere to introduce a daily profit-and-loss statement, a detailed report ranging from such vital matters as every single penny spent for food to the prevailing state of the weather.

Hilton wages continuous war on waste. He contends that one reason so many hotels lose money is that their eyes are shut to so many golden opportunities to turn waste into money. He says they can't "visualize." Particularly keen on making profitable use of "dead" space, his lively imagination serves him well. He has a "see-ing eye," and when he walks into a new hotel he has just acquired, things begin to happen right off. Are guests not patronizing that gift shop near the entrance? Then out with it! In the Palmer House, for example, when Hilton found the barbershop serving patrons none too well and losing money to boot, he took it away from the concessionaire and put it in charge of the hotel management. In the Stevens, a completely dead area on the Eighth Street side now houses a profitable men's taproom; a blank wall was broken into to make room for an Eastern Airlines ticket office; another airline, PCA, was provided space by the removal of the general cashier's window to a less valuable location; and the cigar stand was combined with the newsstand to make room for TWA. Such changes as these not only bring in new revenue, but improve the service to the guests.

The Plaza Hotel in New York is a striking example of the Hilton brand of imagination. It was on the rocks when Hilton took it over. The old owners declared it couldn't make money, but Hilton, the visualizer, allowed that it could, and the deal was closed.

The ground floor was surveyed, new entrances made, walls shifted around, valuable new spaces created. The ground floor offices of E. F. Hutton & Company were moved to what had been completely nonproductive space on the mezzanine floor, a change that turned out to be to their sales advantage. Into the new spaces went a smart and spacious cocktail lounge and fashionable new shops; among the occupants are Elizabeth Arden, Hattie Carnegie, Rosemarie, and John Rubel, the jeweler. Thirty-five thousand dollars were spent to give the old Palm Court a new *décor*. These changes increased the ground floor income by $150,000, alone enough to have saved the Plaza for the old owners if they had only "visualized."

Hating waste, impatient with cumbersome, old-fashioned methods, Hilton spent $150,000 to modernize the antique Plaza kitchen. No detail was overlooked, even to such things as decreasing the sharp angle of the stairway to make it easier on waiters and bus boys. So it went all over the place, on every floor, in every department, and when Hilton had finished he had spent $3,000,000 to put the run-down plant into shape. But it was all in the interest of moneymaking business efficiency, all in pursuit of the dominant Hilton idea that the only really good hotel is the hotel that runs at a profit.

"Visualization" is a sort of hobby with Hilton. It is a word that is constantly bobbing up in his conversation. Gazing at a dreary stretch of ocean sand, he sees big umbrellas in gay colors and lovely maidens plunging into the water. He seems to do it instinctively, almost without thinking. Consider the case of the Breakers, at Long Beach, California. The place had been closed for six years, a tax burden of $280,000 breaking its back. Hotel men, bankers, even speculators, would have nothing to do with it; they said it never could be made to pay. Yet Hilton made it into one of the greatest money-makers in the country.

One day, while examining the building, Hilton (quoting his own words) "visualized what a Sky Room, looking out over the Pacific Ocean, would be." So orders were issued, orders to gut the entire top floor. The result was the Hilton Sky Room, one of the most successful rooms of its kind in the history of the hotel business. Almost overnight the Breakers, now named the Hilton, began to pay dividends.

It is obvious that Hilton's purchase of the Breakers took courage. And so did the purchase of the Roosevelt, which had not paid a dividend in eighteen years. Hilton's courage springs from his imagination. His power to envision himself as having triumphantly achieved his objectives, his peculiar faculty for forming mental pictures of what happily lies ahead, is the explanation of his never-say-die spirit.

In his earlier days Hilton survived many heartbreaking crises. On one occasion he hurried at night to the home of a postmaster, begged him for the return of a check that had accidentally been mailed too soon. Hilton's bank account was down to zero, and he knew the check would bounce back. The postmaster, affected by Hilton's earnestness and enthusiasm about his future, not only returned the letter but loaned him enough money to stave off the sheriff.

This enthusiasm of Hilton's is extremely contagious. It is reflected in the ardor, competency, and complete loyalty of his staff from top to bottom. His managers without exception seem to have been cast in the same mold. He has an uncanny ability for picking men skilled not only in the arts of sound business practice, but skilled, too, in the Hilton art of "visualizing."

But they are not yes men. Hilton gives his managers plenty of authority to act on their own. After he bought the nearly defunct Roosevelt, he flew back home to California, wired the manager of his El Paso hotel to fly to New York and take charge of the newly acquired headache. That was in February; Hilton didn't see his new hostelry until the following June. But the back-country boy from Texas was doing all right. Past debts had been paid off and dividends had been resumed.

Hilton's conception of hospitality is the kind of courtesy and friendliness one would expect in a well-managed bank. He believes guests are eager to feel that they are welcome, that their patronage is appreciated, but that they don't want to be pawed over, have their backs slapped. Hilton does not believe that "bigness" is in itself an attraction. When he bought the Stevens it was advertised as the "world's largest." He at once gave orders to his advertising agency to include "and friendliest" in every advertisement. When he bought the Town House, then half empty, it was the policy of the management never to ask the public for its patronage. Clerks were never permitted to quote prices. Hilton changed that in a hurry. He ran ads, dignified but friendly, inviting everybody to come in and see what he had to offer and quoting prices that "challenged comparison." In no time at all the house was sold out.

Hilton loves his business. A big, tanned man with a big, boyish grin, he likes people and is happiest when he is busily planning better ways to be a better host. He is unhappiest when Hilton service falls short of what he feels his guests expect. No form letters are used to answer complaints. Hilton personally writes a sincere and friendly note to every complaining guest, and he loses no time in correcting the cause of the trouble.

Hilton has tremendous energy, works hard, and operates when necessary on four hours' sleep a day. But, more than anything else, what built the Hilton empire is the impelling force and reach of the man's imagination.

When a businessman originates an idea that represents a departure from old ways, when he makes a clean break with tradition and often with prejudice, put it down that he has performed an act of real imagination. Only the faculty of imagination can break the bonds that fetter men to rutted ways of thinking. Always there have been restless, curious, meditative men forever looking for better ways of doing things, and their businesses have prospered because their ideas have been of genuine service to mankind. Opportunity awaits the creative thinker in every field of human activity. "There is no limit," said Henry Ward Beecher, "to the sphere of ideas."

3

Imagination Gives You Courage

In Chapter Two you read how imagination built for Conrad N. Hilton his vast hotel empire, how, starting from scratch twenty-seven years ago, he made himself the most spectacular figure in United States hotel history.

It is obvious that great courage and stubborn determination played a vital part in Hilton's success. In the Roosevelt he bought a hotel that hadn't paid a dividend in eighteen years. In the Breakers he acquired a hotel that had been closed for six years and that carried a load of $250,000 in back taxes. The Plaza was a dead horse and bankers and hotel men would have nothing to do with it. The Stevens, considered by many too far from Chicago's Loop, had a bad financial history and businessmen shook their heads pessimistically when Hilton bought the huge hostelry.

What was said in Chapter Two will easily bear repeating: Hilton's courage springs from his imagination. His power to envision himself as having triumphantly achieved his objective, his peculiar faculty for forming mental pictures of what happily lies ahead, is the explanation of his never-say-die spirit.

Many men and women in business are timid, overcautious, afraid to take a chance. They consider a plan for altering and enlarging their stores or their factories, or adding a branch office in another city, or hiring two or three additional salesmen, or adding a new line of merchandise, or doubling their advertising investment, or whatever, only to lose confidence in the end and give up their dreams of expansion.

What such people lack is imagination. It goes without saying, of course, that reckless overexpansion is a very bad thing, but it is also true that overconservatism is equally fatal to progressive growth in business.

The imaginative man projects his thoughts into the future. He sees ahead. He dreams. He may own nothing but a little repair shop on a back street, but once his imagination has got up a full head of steam, he can see painted on the canvas of his mind a picture of a fine, big two-story garage equipped with an ever-ringing cash register. He is not easily discouraged, readily visualizes himself as overcoming obstacles, winning out over setbacks, achieving "impossible" objectives.

My good friend, the late Martin L. Davey, was a man of remarkable imagination and courage. In addition to being a prominent political figure, he was for many years president of The Davey Tree Expert Company, of Kent, Ohio. His father, John Davey, an English emigrant having neither money nor formal education, was passionately obsessed with the idea that ailing and wounded trees could be saved by scientific care. His book *The Tree Doctor* aroused widespread interest; but John Davey was not interested in commerce, and his new science of tree surgery as a business enterprise made slow progress.

In those early days young Martin was working his way through Oberlin College peddling typewriters and doing tree surgery in his spare time. Out of school, he decided to make his father's idea his lifework, and it was three or four years after this when I met him. He was doing a little advertising through the Thompson advertising agency and I met him in connection with this work.

Martin Davey didn't have much in the way of assets beyond John Davey's book and a handful of customers. But he had imagination. He had dreams. He talked big, looked ahead to the time when he would have branch sales offices in every important city and two thousand expert tree surgeons at work—saving America's beautiful trees.

He wanted to spend five thousand dollars for the year's advertising—a small sum indeed as advertising appropriations go, but a very large sum for his little company of tree surgeons.

I recall asking if he thought the expenditure was wise, for he had told me that he had scarcely enough money in the bank to meet his small pay roll. "I can't fail," he replied. "Just use your imagination, man! Think of all the beautiful country estates in America, and think of their lovely, priceless trees, generations old and many of them dying, and think of how they are prized by their owners! There is a big, potential business waiting for me. I can feel it. I can see it just as vividly as if it existed right now."

Well, Martin Davey's imagination gave him courage. He persuaded the local bank to make a small loan, he borrowed a thousand dollars or so on his life insurance, the agency extended him a little credit, and he told me to go ahead with the advertising.

The advertising paid off, not spectacularly, but it produced enough demand for the Davey service to justify a slightly larger expenditure in the following year. For five or six of those early pioneering years the road was rocky. There never was quite enough capital to make advertising expenditures an easy decision, and a man of lesser imagination—hence lesser courage—would never have achieved Martin Davey's fine success.

The man of imagination sees his goals clearly marked on the road ahead, and he sets out with a sure instinct in their direction. Because he is so sure of himself, so certain about his objectives, he marches forward sturdily with a courageous heart.

This brings me to the story of a boy named Gene who, when he was still in short pants, decided that he was, fundamentally, a mechanic. His family's finances were such that he had to get out and hustle.

He resolved at the very outset that his hustling would be confined strictly to such work as would further his great ambition. He knew exactly what he was after: he wanted to learn mechanics and he wanted eventually to be his own boss in a business making and selling mechanical things. So, logically enough, he and a schoolboy friend went into the doorbell business.

Electric doorbells were then just coming into general use and many installations were not satisfactory. Gene and his schoolmate went up and down the streets pushing doorbells. If the bell failed to ring, or if there were a sign on the door, "Bell out of order," which was often the case, the boys would knock, point out the bell's failure, and offer to put it into first-class condition. At homes having no electric bells, the two young mechanics would do their best to sell a new installation.

The little business was a money-maker, but Gene wasn't content: he knew his knowledge of mechanics was too meager. He quit the little firm, put on his Sunday suit, and went to the Franklin Automobile Company for a job. The factory superintendent, grinning sardonically at the boy's nice clothes and gloved hands, put him to work filing castings in assembly—a nasty chore which was a sort of hazing to weed out the weaklings. But the lad was a die-hard and stuck it out. Soon he was given a chance to work at assembling engines—a task he became so good at that in a few months he was the prize assembler in the plant.

Now Gene was ready for his next move: if he was eventually to boss a company of his own he would have to learn something about selling and business. Screwing up his courage, he went to the general manager of the plant and told him he wanted a job selling the Franklin car. He told the manager that he had qualified himself in the factory, that he would sell with enthusiasm because he knew firsthand the quality which was built into each Franklin, and that when Franklins broke down on the road, as all cars did in those days, he could make them run again. In spite of his extreme youth Gene got the job. Now he was really on his way.

Today the one-time doorbell tinkerer, Eugene F. McDonald, Jr., is president of his own company, the Zenith Radio Corporation. He is still tinkering faithfully with things mechanical, as has been his habit for forty years, and he has achieved to the full his boyhood ambition. I know Eugene McDonald well, and it is my settled conviction that the source of his strength and his courage is the scope and intensity of his remarkable imagination.

You will find inspiration in this story about a lad named Eddie. When he was fourteen years old his mind was made up: the gasoline engine was to be his lifework.

The automobile was a primitive contraption then, and the horse still king of the highway. People laughed at the boy's strange ambition. No matter; his imagination was afire: he was looking ahead.

The odor of burning oil was to his nostrils what the delightful fragrance of printer's ink is to the printer, and at last his ardor was rewarded: he got a job—which paid him six dollars a week—as general helper in a little garage, and here he picked up a smattering of the elementary knowledge of mechanics he craved so much.

There was a small automobile factory in his town of Columbus, Ohio, and for month after month he hounded its chief engineer, Lee Frayer, for a chance to work under him. Again and again Frayer said no; his lack of interest in the supplications of the eager-eyed youth was relentless.

Then one day Eddie noticed how badly Frayer's machine shop needed a general cleaning. "Listen, Mr. Frayer," said Eddie, "I am going to be on the job at seven o'clock in the morning whether or not you pay me."

The offer left Frayer cold, and he impatiently shooed the lad out of the shop. But the next morning die-hard Eddie, back with a broom, a brush, and a shovel, went to work. Half of the shop was clean when Frayer arrived—and the astonished man was so bowled over by the difference between the clean half of the place and the dirty half that he hired the youngster on the spot.

The remainder of the story you'll find in *Who's Who*: how Eddie—whose full name is E. V. Rickenbacker climbed to the heights as a spectacular automobile-racing driver, as a renowned flying ace in World War I, as the founder of an automobile company, as an outstanding pioneer and leader in civilian air transportation, and as the president and general manager (his job today) of Eastern Air Lines.

As a boy Rickenbacker was desperately poor, but he refused chances to make money in other kinds of work. His imagination told him what he wanted—and it gave him the courage to get it. Opportunities in other fields have beckoned him, but for more than forty years he has been loyal to his one great obsession, the gasoline engine, and the world has made way for him.

You can see from what you have just read that not only does imagination give you courage, but it is the only thing under the sun that will. When things go badly, it's easy for even the most stouthearted among us to quail. That's natural.

One of my (Woolf) young friends, an ex-serviceman in business for himself for the first time, ran into hard going right off the reel. He hadn't counted on that: he thought his dreams would be rosy right from the start. But they weren't. He faced bleak days: it was doubtful if he could keep his store open another twenty-four hours.

Fortunately, he weathered the storm, is now in a thriving way. When I met him on the street the other day he told me, "There's only one thing that kept me going during those hard, hard months you know I had."

"What was it?"

"Faith in my destiny," he replied.

"What do you mean?" I wasn't quite clear from his words, but I thought I knew what he was driving at.

"Simply this: When things were the darkest, I would keep in front of my eyes the picture that I had when I went into business— the happy picture of being a successful businessman, of having a big house of my own, several cars, ease, success.

"I would tell myself that these hard lines of my present weren't my life at all," he continued. "I saw myself away from these hard times, out in the open of ease and independence. And only that gave me the courage to keep on—only that picture I kept before me kept me in business."

Don't you see what this youngster was doing? He was using imagination to give himself courage. He was imagining himself in the position he wanted to be in: he was seeing beyond the door of the present into the future. And anyone who can and will do that can keep on going regardless of how strait the present may be.

I recollect what an old man told me years ago, when a period of discouragement had come to me, about keeping sight of the big goal—that is, using imagination.

"Got fifty cents?" he requested.

"Yes."

"All right. Hold it up close to your eye, thus," describing how to hold a fifty-cent piece as if it were a monocle.

I did as instructed.

"Close your other eye. Can you see the sun?"

"How do you expect me to see the sun with one eye closed and a half dollar in front of the other one?" I wanted to know.

"Then the half dollar is bigger than the sun, isn't it?" he observed. "It's so big it hides out the sun."

What he was telling me is that unless I had imagination to project myself into the future, I could be beaten by any little obstacle that came along, but that if I would use imagination, see things in their true perspective, nothing that could happen could be big enough to daunt me.

Men who have made good on their own, often after fruitless attempts, all agree that it's always too soon to quit. They hang on a little bit longer, often with nothing more than imagination to sustain them and give them courage.

If you had the case records of successful men or businesses you'd be astonished at how many of both of them were on the verge of failure when success finally came.

"Only a fool would have done what I did," one of the most successful men I have known said to me just the other day. "Only a fool would have hung on as long as I did. I was whipped. My family knew it. My associates knew it. My banker knew it. My creditors knew it. I knew it. But I hung on anyway. I stayed on for a little while longer—and won. I couldn't quit."

"Why couldn't you?" I asked him.

"My imagination wouldn't let me," he said, seriously. "I knew I could win because I kept carrying in my mind's eye a success picture that was just too beautiful and too realistic for me to blot out."

And that is the story of every successful man I have told you about in this chapter. It is the story of Conrad Hilton, of Martin Davey, of Eddie Rickenbacker, of Gene McDonald. They all had moments when their dreams seemed doomed, but because they were, to a man, filled with imagination their dreams were bigger, stronger than anything that could happen. They and their imaginations won!

4
NEW LIFE FOR AILING BUSINESSES

When a man can take a large city bank which, even after fifty-one years of operation, has total resources of only eight million dollars, and in three years quadruple those figures, at the same time doubling the number of its customers; when the same man—despite an organized financial bloc which had such a close hold on the banking business in the town that it was virtually impossible for an outsider to get a foothold—can make his bank the most popular in the city; when he is so far ahead in his thinking that bankers all over the country consult him and follow his lead, there must be something so fundamentally right about this man's methods that it would pay anyone to know what it is.

This is what Elwood M. Brooks, a small-town banker from Kansas, did when he invaded the big time by becoming president of a stagnating, run-down bank in Denver, Colorado.

Mr. Brooks hadn't ever had a day's experience with a big city bank, didn't know big-city banking problems, so the odds were against him. Besides, in selecting Denver for his operations he selected one of the hardest of all American cities. For twenty years the banks in Denver had been held in the firm grasp of a hide-bound, complacent, stuffy group of financial interests that were not interested in progress, but only in keeping their strangle hold on the town. Moreover, the bank bought by Mr. Brooks and his associates had slipped back so far it was doubtful if anything could be done to revive it; for when a bank is dead it is deader than any other business on earth.

This was the picture into which Elwood Brooks stepped, and almost anyone could have told him how impossible his job was. To offset his lack of city experience and to help him overcome those insuperable obstacles you have just read about, he had on his side only one asset. But what an asset! It is something that works equally well in big cities or in little cities, in banks or in butcher-shops, in law offices or in lapidaries.

He had *imagination*.

The story of Elwood Brooks and the Central Bank and Trust Company is a triumph of imagination, and a saga of encouragement for anyone who has an ailing business on his hands into which he wishes to breathe new life. Let me (Roth) tell the story as Elwood Brooks told it to me not long ago.

"I wasn't too sure I had any business trying to be a big-city banker," Mr. Brooks began. "All my experience had been in the country with small-town banks. But I had an idea. My idea was this: if I could run a bank for the little fellow—for the man in the street—for the man who is awed by the cold austerity usually found in big banks, he would respond to my friendliness just as the people in the country always did."

That's when Mr. Brooks' imagination started to work—when he thought of running a bank for the little fellow.

His first step was to place his desk out in the lobby, where he would be available during every business day for anyone who wanted to see him. His next step was to put some of his ideas into motion.

Denver woke up one morning to realize that there was a new note in Denver banking—a full-page advertisement in the newspaper announced an entirely new service: pay-as-you-go checking accounts, which required no minimum balance. And after that came a succession of new ideas, startling ideas, in rapid-fire order. The first was the "Thrifty Way Purchase Plan" accounts, by which you could save enough for whatever you wanted and then pay for it in advance—a little put away each week. Then came a Veterans' Advisory Department . . . then loans on airplanes . . . then a Home Planning Institute . . . then banking by mail . . . then music in the bank!

It seemed that every week the Central Bank had something new up its sleeve to spring on Denver—and Denver responded in exactly the same way that everyone responds to good ideas. It yielded the Central Bank its confidence and business. Witness the growth in three years' time from resources of $8,000,000 to resources of $35,000,000!

Where did Elwood Brooks get all these ideas that worked such wonders? He didn't just dream them up in the way of a poet composing a sonnet. He followed the route which you have read about in this book—the route of analysis and synthesis. You will recollect that in Chapter Two you read that analysis is a taking apart, while synthesis is a putting together. This is the way Mr. Brooks came by his ideas:

"For four years I was State Bank Commissioner in Kansas," he told me. "I watched over the operation of five hundred banks. Some of these made rapid progress. Some stood still.

"I studied the methods of the banks that were making progress [analysis] and compared them with the methods of the banks that were standing still. What was the difference? Invariably the banks that went ahead were banks that offered ideas—that brought new services, new conveniences, new angles to their patrons. I began taking the ideas I had seen in use and applying them mentally [synthesis] to a big-city bank. Long before I opened for business in Denver, I had a blueprint of what I was going to do."

Let me give you a little more detail of the kind of ideas Elwood Brooks used in turning an "impossible" banking situation into a success story of satisfaction and profit.

He was the first in Denver to offer pay-as-you-go checking accounts, requiring a payment of ten cents per check for every check written—no minimum balance. He was the first to establish a practical department exclusively devoted to handling livestock loans. He was the first to open a Veterans' Advisory Department to give financial advice to returning GIs; he was also the first to advertise veterans' loans.

He was the first to install a consumers' loan department as a distinct and separate division of the bank to lend money to the little fellow. He advertised loans on airplanes months in advance of anyone else. He was the first to offer free parking to patrons. He was the first to advertise a "bank by mail" offer.

He was the first banker in the city with a "Hurry Up Depository"—for depositors who are in too much of a hurry to stand in line for the teller to take their deposit: they merely drop it in a chute in the lobby, their account is credited, their book returned.

He was the first to install music in the bank for the enjoyment of customers, the first to participate in a Home Planning Institute, the first to offer his customers a "Thrifty Way Purchase Plan," which enables the customers to start saving to buy the things he had as his postwar dreams—a new car, a refrigerator, a vacuum cleaner, even a home.

I have gone into detail in giving the story of Elwood Brooks and his Central Bank, because it points up what I wish to dwell on in this chapter: namely, that whenever a business starts going downhill, the reason is usually a lack of ideas—and that the only way the business can be put back on the upgrade is by introducing new ideas into its operations.

I suppose you have noticed that whenever a business changes hands, you will usually find a sign in the window reading: *Open for business—under new management*. That sign usually advertises that the old management was deficient in ideas and consequently went broke and that the new management hopes to do better with ideas. And often it works out that way, and many an old, ailing business has been put back on its feet by a fresh start (fresh ideas, that is) under new management.

But it isn't necessary to have a new management to have new ideas, and if any business now ailing can be infused with new ideas, no matter how far gone the business may be, I think it can be reestablished as a going concern.

The easiest thing in the world when a business is going along successfully is to let down in the matter of ideas. That is not only easy, but also natural, for the attitude of everyone is to let well enough alone.

One of the best examples I know of a fine business that was sacked because the founder turned it over to unimaginative persons to run (while she let down on having ideas and took her ease) is that of Alice Foote MacDougall. This is what happened, in Mrs. MacDougall's own words:

"My husband was in the coffee business, and it was a man's business. When he became very ill and couldn't possibly work any more, I realized it was up to me. I went down to his office and took over. Many a night I got home sure that I'd ruined everything. But I kept at it, and after a while, as I got more confidence and began putting more ideas to work, things went pretty well.

"I had an idea I could advertise my coffee by opening a little restaurant in Grand Central Station, in New York. I opened one. I had ideas, so my place in Grand Central was so popular that six months later I opened a second restaurant.

"In five years I had six large restaurants that were crowded from morning till night. I was taking in two million dollars a year through the restaurants—and making another half million selling coffee and china. I lived on Park Avenue. I had everything I could possibly want.

"One day in 1930, I thought, 'things are going well. I'm sixty-three. I've worked long enough. Why not call it a day?' So I gave up control of my business and settled back to what I thought was going to be a life of ease.

"Well, it was fine while it lasted. But everything went wrong. The crowds stopped eating at Alice Foote MacDougall's. Debt piled up. Then one day the MacDougall restaurants failed. I tried to save them—but it was too late. My savings vanished. The beautiful furnishings in my apartment were sold one by one. A few months ago I had to move to a much smaller place, and just last week the last of my furniture was sold.

"I'm seventy-three years old now. But I'm not through. I'm going to open a place like the one I had at Grand Central so many years ago. I'm going to start over and build as I did once before. I know I can do it, because, you see, I still have ideas!"

And build Mrs. MacDougall did. If death hadn't intervened when she was just getting a foothold on her second business career, there's little doubt that she would have established herself as strongly as she was before. The domain of ideas, you see, is not the possession of those who are young, or middle-aged, or old; and if any man or woman can have ideas, keep on having ideas, he or she is never too old to cure an ailing business or start a new one.

Take the story of H. Tom Collard. Here is a man who, because of his genius for ideas, took a manufacturer's error and turned it into a nationally successful business—although he himself was flat broke when the error occurred. Mr. Collard was fifty at the time and "dead, stony-broke. Not even two Lincoln heads to rub together—and that's being broke!" He was operating a small rubber firm. An eastern rubber manufacturer shipped him a pail of latex by mistake. Mr. Collard didn't need the latex, didn't want it, couldn't pay for it; but when he complained, the manufacturer wrote, "Don't send it back. We will not pay the charges."

So there he was, dead broke, no money, and the last of his slim capital tied up in the express charges on a useless pail of latex. But Tom Collard never was a man to brood. He used his mind for more positive things—to have ideas. He set to work, his lively imagination roving for ways to turn this latex to account. Presently he brought forth a latex cement. Automobile body builders found it useful in their trim departments. Next he developed an idea for spraying latex and invented a special spray gun for the purpose. Inside of six years this man who was "dead, stony-broke" was handling thirty-five tank cars of rubber sap a year, and he was prosperous.

But he wasn't through with his ideas. His next one was to line tanks with sprayed-on latex, compounded for vulcanization. Next came plated and chemical tanks, thousands of which are being used in every part of the country. Came then new products—industrial safety products, a nonslip rug underlay, and many, many others—and Collard's firm was large and prosperous. It just shows what can be done with ideas.

Why, if you have enough ideas of the right kind you can even make a "Jonah" business prosperous. Near my office there is a restaurant which is in that category—a Jonah business. Fifteen different owners have tried to make a go of it. Fifteen owners failed, lost their savings. Then a young chap I know decided he'd give it a whirl; but first he came to me for advice. Knowing the reputation of the place, I advised caution.

"You know what has happened to that restaurant during the past ten years, don't you?" I asked.

"I know exactly. I went into its past history thoroughly."

"What makes you think you can make a go of it when these other dozen or fifteen restaurant men flopped?" I asked.

"Well, I have a lot of ideas of what I believe I can do with the place. Want to hear some of them?"

He outlined a dozen ideas he wanted to put into use, and when he finished I told him to go ahead. He did. I am glad to say that he was on the upgrade inside of three months and now, two years later, his place is packed night and day. And what kind of ideas did he use in working this miracle? Not complicated, expensive ideas, but just everyday things that his imagination showed him the workingmen who patronized a restaurant in that neighborhood would like—thicker slices of bread than they get in other places, larger cups of coffee, a jar of honey on the table all the time, hot biscuits at dinner in the evening, and homemade pie in place of soggy, baker's pie.

Let us assume that your own business isn't doing as well as you would like and that you are wondering how you can apply this miracle of imagination to improving it. Just how shall you go about it?

These are my suggestions: *First, find out the greatest need of the business.*

Do you need more customers, larger orders, more efficient production, expanded markets, or just what? It seems to me you should ascertain that first, because then you will know how to slant your ideas. Carry this question around in your mind for a few days. The answer may come to you before very long.

One of my friends took this advice three years ago when his jewelry store was going sour on him. After mulling it over for two weeks he decided that what he needed more than anything else was new customers. He had been in business for many, many years and had a good clientele. But his customers were most of them old. One by one they were retiring and moving away or dying, and his business was virtually drying up.

When he saw the need, the rest was easy. He began getting ideas for appealing to the younger element in the community. He advertised lower cost merchandise to attract those of smaller incomes.

He made the store a pleasant place for these youngsters to trade in. He put into use such ideas as gifts for the babies if their mothers would bring them in, special jewelry for teen-agers, and other attractions for the new customers he needed. The result was a completely rejuvenated business in three years' time.

The next thing, once you decide the greatest need of your business, is to *ask yourself how this need can be met.*

You see, when you think in terms of ideas, you get much farther if you aim at a definite target than if you merely day-dream and do wishful thinking. See if you can aim some of your ideas at this need of yours; be positive and honest with yourself about it.

Turn your imagination loose.

Make a list of every possible idea you can think of that bears on your problem. List them all, no matter how silly they sound to you. When I say list them, I mean just that—put them down.

One of my friends, now head of a chain store organization in Texas, was a few years ago called in to retrieve a small, ailing business which belonged to a member of the family. He followed the process I'm outlining for you: he ascertained the need, he tried to see how the need could be met, he got as many ideas for meeting it as he could.

For several weeks he walked around just thinking up ideas, all kinds of ideas—wild ideas, tame ideas, practical ideas, impractical ideas. Whenever one came to him, no matter where he was, he put it down in a little black book he carried with him night and day. In all, he had over a hundred ideas. He didn't need a fifth of that number, because the business was soon on its way up, and a chain organization, noticing the master hand of ideas at work, bought up the business in order to get the services of my friend.

Now go through your ideas and work out a timetable for putting them into effect.

Some of your ideas you can put to use at once; others will have to wait. Put those you can use into effect as soon as you can, but salt the others away for some future use. It is a good idea to work out a definite timetable and keep it in front of you, so that you will never let yourself sag in this matter of putting new ideas to work for you.

One of the things which I believe helped John D. Rockefeller attain such greatness was this habit of his of putting ideas on a timetable basis. Once he was discussing with his son an idea of which he was particularly fond.

"It will be twenty-five years before we can start using that idea in our business," he told the son. "But that's all right. We have other ideas we can begin using at once."

He was looking ahead a quarter of a century until conditions would be right for the use of an idea in which he believed.

You need not plan so far ahead, but you should have plenty of ideas for both times, the present and the future, so that you will never be caught short in the matter of ideas.

Now my next suggestion: *Go on a new-idea-a-week basis.*

It doesn't sound like a very formidable task to have just one new idea a week for the good of your business. But do you realize that if you can introduce just an idea a week you will have fifty-two new ideas working for you at the end of your first year? And any business would prosper mightily with a transfusion of this kind in its veins every year.

Although it sounds simple to have one idea a week, one new idea a week, you might find after a few weeks that it isn't nearly so simple as it sounds. One of my friends, sales manager for a large firm, had a salesman on his staff who wasn't making the grade. He called the boy in for a talk.

"The trouble with you, Bob," he began, "is that you aren't putting enough new ideas into your work. Here is what I want you to do: Every Monday morning I want you to show up with one new idea—any kind of an idea—for increasing the sale of our product in your territory. One idea a week is all I ask of you. Do you think you can do that?"

"One idea a week? Only one idea a week?" the salesman responded. "Sure, boss. If you had wanted an idea a day I could have done that, too. But one idea a week is duck soup."

"All right. Let's see you do it."

For the first two weeks, my friend says, the salesman dutifully had his ideas, but then he began to sag. At the end of a month he had to confess he simply could not produce an idea a week for increasing business. It was too much for him.

He had no imagination, that salesman, and did not deserve to succeed. But another friend of mine did have imagination. He operates a lettershop. It got into the doldrums, seemed fit to fail, when he called his staff together and told them:

"We are a bunch of nitwits, that is what we are. Here we are in an idea business, selling ideas to other people for increasing their business—and how long has it been since we have had one idea for increasing our own?"

He was met with silence.

"From now on," he continued, "from now on, each of us is going to show up here on Saturday morning with one idea for increasing the business of this lettershop. There are ten of us. That will be ten ideas a week—five hundred ideas a year. I'll bet we can whip this thing if we can give ourselves ideas like that. Are you game?"

They all were. It took just exactly three months to put that business on an even keel. Today it is ten times as large as it was when he and his associates started on their idea-a-week basis.

The rest of the job of reviving an ailing business by the use of ideas is simply to put the good ideas into practice—and then never to stop having ideas. For the minute you believe you can operate a business without new ideas all the time you start running head-on into trouble. Certainly what Harvey Firestone said just before he died is true: "Capital isn't so important in business. Experience isn't so important. You can get both those things. What is important is ideas. If you have ideas, you have the main asset you need, and there isn't any limit to what you can do with your business and your life. They are any man's greatest asset—ideas."

5
Employers Listen to the Man with an Idea

Unless an employer has a definite job to offer an applicant, he is likely to turn him away with the response "I'm sorry, but we don't need anyone right now."

If this happens to you, don't forget that the employer may be mistaken. For often there is a job just waiting for somebody with imagination to come along and create it.

This is a lesson I (Woolf) learned as a boy. Anxious to earn extra money, I asked all three drugstores in my town for a job—any kind, of job. There were no openings. But a week later I found that one of these stores had taken on a new boy. Screwing up my courage, I asked the owner why.

"Well, I'll tell you, son," he said. "I didn't *think* I had a job open when you asked for one. But then Freddie came in with an idea. He owns a bicycle, and he suggested that I start a delivery service, meaning himself. That's a new notion for this town. It's going to make a hit."

Well, I had a bicycle, too, but Freddie had something I didn't have—an idea.

A friend of mine, for many years the successful sports editor of a big Pennsylvania daily, also *thought* himself into his first job. He wanted to be a newspaperman, but the only paper in his small town turned him down. So he started to study the paper for weak spots. Presently he settled on its almost total lack of sporting news and its meager coverage of farm happenings.

Seven days later the young fellow went back with two ideas—and a fistful of copy to back them up. It had been a busy sports week: two high-school ball games, an amusing horseshoe-pitching contest, and horse races at the county fair. He handed the editor a brisk account of these events as the pattern for a sports column. Then he suggested another column, "Farm Doings," for a collection of items he had picked up from farmers. He was hired on the spot.

Recently a lad in Iowa, back from war work in California, got his start by *making* it. A good mechanic, he tackled the owner of a garage. No job! But the youngster didn't give up: he had an idea. He offered to help around the place without pay. The owner said he didn't mind.

The garage had only one repair truck; hence many calls from stranded motorists were turned down. The unpaid helper fixed up a broken-down motorcycle with a sidecar and loaded it with tools for emergency repair jobs. The owner, pleased, gave this returned war worker a well-paying job.

Simple ideas? Maybe so. But consider this fact: During more than thirty years as an advertising agency executive I have interviewed at least five thousand job hunters—and not more than fifty of them came up with even the simplest idea that applied to problems we were talking about.

When scouting for ideas, make a habit of observing *critically* jobs that are being poorly done. The indifference of others may spell opportunity for you. Take, for instance, the case of a man who started life carrying newspapers in Paterson, New Jersey. He noticed that boys who distributed handbills for stores threw them around so carelessly that most of them were wasted.

"How much more profitable it would be," the lad thought, "if each circular were handed to the housewife at the door." He took this idea to the owner of a new store about to open in Paterson— and got the job of distributing his announcements.

The youngster spent four days distributing fliers that another boy would have handled in one day. But on the morning of the opening, there was such a rush of business that the store nearly had to close its doors. The newsboy was hired. Four months later, at the age of sixteen (believe it or not!) he was asked to manage another store in the chain. Today that newsboy, T. J. Grassey, is president of Great Eastern Stores—sixty-three of them.

Then there is the inspiring story of Errett Grable. The salaried job he had been promised blew up; it was to have been his upon his graduation from college. He looked elsewhere, but times were bad, and his diploma didn't mean a thing to hard-pressed employers. Finally he got a chance to sell aluminum cooking utensils door-to-door on commission, and he grabbed it.

But it wasn't exactly the job of Errett Grable's campus dreams. How, he wondered, can I make my new employer take quick notice of me? I am competing with hundreds of other fellows in the field force. Pondering his problem, Errett decided not to try to sell himself to his employers. Instead, he would sell them ideas.

He studied the company's product; he studied the needs and notions of the housewives who bought it. After a few weeks the utensil company began getting letters from young Grable suggesting ways to give better service to customers. His ideas included an improved spout for a teakettle, a new type of order blank to give customers more accurate information, a better way of packing to insure safer delivery of utensils. The frequency and persistency of Grable's letters interested the management, and before long he was called to the home office to fill an opening, a salaried job, as sales correspondent. There the continued submission of business-building ideas paid off for Errett M. Grable: today he is president of the firm, the Aluminum Cooking Utensil Company, one of the largest businesses of its kind in America.

The moral is plain: A sales correspondent was needed—with hundreds of hard-working young men in the field force to choose from. The call went out to the one among them who had proved the quality of his imagination. It happens so often that way in business. Employers listen to the man with ideas.

Remember that your idea needs to be original only in its application to your prospective employer's business. Johnston's county survey plan may have been an old one in Cincinnati or South Bend, but it was as new as a fresh-minted coin to the bankers of Lebanon. And that was what counted.

Here is another story of how a young student engineer from Kalamazoo created an opportunity for himself. Arriving in Detroit "broke, up to my ears in debt, and out of a job," Howard Blood turned to the want ads, found a chance to do time-study work for the Detroit Gear and Machine Company. It wasn't what he had hoped for, but it was a living.

A third floor was being added to the building, and it called for a complete and difficult reshuffle of the facilities of the whole plant. Young Blood, saying nothing, quietly studied the problem, dreamed up an idea. Working, in his odd moments, with penknife and saw, scissors and paper and string, he began building a scale-model skeleton structure of the plant. Beams and uprights were small sticks of wood; machines and men, material and products, were little colored-paper cutouts; and vari-hued strings indicated the flow of production.

One day the general manager peeped over Howard's shoulder. "What's that, young man?" he asked.

"It's an idea on visualizing a factory layout so you can see exactly how it will operate on a full-scale basis."

In those days (1915) that *was* a new idea. Within a few days Howard, despite his youth, was made production manager and put in full charge of the new plant arrangement. An employee of the factory for only a few weeks, he won, thanks to an idea, a promotion that ordinarily might have been years in coming, if at all. Howard E. Blood's imagination has since carried him far up the ladder: today he is president of the Norge Division of Borg-Warner Corporation.

Getting a job is largely a matter of selling; the man who is doing the hiring must see you, listen to you, be interested, be convinced. Try to think up a way of dramatizing yourself—but don't despair if you can't originate a brand new idea of your own. Borrow from others: adapt to your problem ideas already proved to be effective. Here's a true story that illustrates the point. In the early nineties a dark young tailor from Poland arrived in New York in search of a job—and an opportunity to demonstrate his skill.

He had great skill; that he knew. But as he went from one dressmaking house to another, the answer was always the same: "You may have great skill as a tailor, but there are no openings here." Weeks passed, but the discouraged job-hunter could not sell himself into a berth. Then an idea came to him: why not hire a living mannequin to wear his suits and thus dramatize what his fine tailoring could do for the feminine figure? After all, Herman reasoned, did not the great Worth of Paris do this? Next day he set out with his lovely mannequin, and in less than a week he had not only a job but one that gave him a great chance to show his skill. Today the young Polish tailor heads the five famous specialty shops which bear his name.

The point to note is this: Herman Milgrim's idea was not really new. He simply applied to job-hunting what he had seen in the smart salons of Worth and other famous Paris designers.

Remember always that the employer has no initial interest in you. It is his major interest and responsibility to see that his business makes money. Give him an idea that will help him do this and watch his eyes sparkle. If you have in mind a particular kind of business, or perhaps have your eyes on a particular concern you would like to be with, read up on it, ask questions, study its problems, talk with consumers, dealers, salesmen, workmen. There was young Ed Thye, for example, back from World War I to find returning job-hungry servicemen walking the streets.

The tractor was just coming into use and young Thye decided he wanted to get into the farm implement business. But it was the old story: no jobs open. Maybe they think they have no jobs, reasoned Ed, but somewhere I'll bet you they have a problem. So he talked to farmers, dealers, county agents, and decided that the new tractors would flop unless they were serviced by factory-trained field men. The small individual farmer didn't know how to keep the darn things running. The Deere plow works couldn't see Ed's idea at first, but he pestered them so doggedly that he was given the go-ahead. He went into the Waterloo factory as a raw mechanic and learned the mysteries of the tractor inside and out. Then, in response to the growing call from farmers for service, Ed took his monkey wrench and went into the field as a tractor expert. Farmers had the welcome mat out. From there he went into the sales department, his original ambition—and he was on his way! Edward J. Thye, who was recently governor of Minnesota, puts it this way: "I realized I had a little selling job to do. I couldn't figure out any reason why the tractor company should be interested in me, but I

knew doggone well that they were mighty interested in any ideas
that would help promote their pioneering young business."

The general manager of a large hardware jobbing company said
to me not long ago: "Today a young chap, a clerk in our sales department, came to me with an idea for simplifying salesmen's reports. I nearly fainted with surprise. Such a thing doesn't happen
once in a blue moon, either among our own help or applicants for
jobs. I don't expect world-shaking suggestions; just little ideas—a
way to save string or wrapping paper, for example—would be welcome. But even such ideas are all too rare."

Homer Adkins' idea, as a case in point, was not world-shaking.
He wanted, desperately, a job in the building materials business
and he wanted it with a certain old and well-established firm. Nothing doing, though—no jobs open. But Homer got his job with a very
simple, obvious idea. He nosed around and found that the company was making no regular calls on architects and contractors to
find out what construction was being planned and that (believe it
or not!) no inspection of building permits was being made. "I want
a job," said Homer to the sleepy old company, "and here is exactly
what it is." He got it.

But that was only the beginning: Homer Adkins was destined
for bigger things. For seven years he served as United States Collector of Internal Revenue, and from 1941 to 1945 as governor of
his home state (Arkansas). Nobody can convince his friends that a
fertile imagination has not been a vital force in his success.

There is inspiration in the story of young Bob Barnett. A poorly
paid clerk in Wall Street when he joined the Marines in World War I,
to be a banker was the great dream of his life. The fighting over,
and now with a wife to support, his old job in the postwar slump
wasn't worth taking, and besides it wasn't in banking.

Bob Barnett realized he must have a plan of strategy. He knew
what he wanted, and now he must know how he intended to get
there. He chose one of the largest banks in New York and decided
that there his destiny awaited him.

But the senior officer of the bank disagreed. The young applicant, after being told to write a letter, was quickly eased out the
door. He wrote the letter, but nothing happened. So back he went,

not once but many times, only to be advised to look elsewhere. He was told that he might (just *might*) find a welcome at another bank down the street.

But the second bank was not interested, and young Barnett made call after call with no results. Finally the officer warmed a little. "Come back," he said, "in three months and maybe we'll have something for you." It was a polite no, and nothing else.

But it didn't mean no to this determined young ex-marine. He resolved that exactly three months from that day he would call again. In the meantime he would have to try to support his family with whatever temporary work he could find. Three months later to the day he was back for that "promised" job. He stood at the officer's desk and refused to budge—and his tenacity won. It wasn't much of a berth, merely the auditing of a pile of dusty old records, and it was strictly on a trial basis of three months. But it was the chance the young fellow had so desperately and stubbornly sought—the momentous first step in the long climb that made Robert E. Barnett the president today of the Irving Savings Bank of New York.

Once there was a Texas boy named Coke who was set on being a lawyer. But his chances looked pretty thin, particularly after family circumstances compelled him to quit school at the age of fourteen.

Coke couldn't find anything to do in a law office, not even sweeping out, so he went to work on a ranch as a handy man. When he was sixteen he quit to drive a freight wagon, a six-horse affair, on a six-day haul over the lone Texas plains between Junction and Brady. At nights around the campfire he studied bookkeeping, figuring that if he had a town job he would have a better chance to learn about law. A year and a half later he drove his last load of freight to Junction and quit.

He had his eyes on the Junction bank, but the bank needed neither bookkeeper nor clerk. "All right," said Coke, "if I can't keep your books I'll scrub your floors and dust your desks." "Okay, son," said the president, "you're hired as a janitor; salary twenty dollars a month." Coke "janitored" for a year and then kept books for four years more, and during every spare minute of that long tedious stretch he studied law. Finally, the boy ranch hand, now twenty-two, was admitted to the bar. It was a victory of the spirit—the die-hard spirit of every successful man who knows what he wants and is stubborn about getting it. Coke Stevenson was recently the governor of the state that gave him his chance—Texas.

Henry L. Mencken's modest account of how he got his start in the newspaper business, the *Baltimore Morning Herald*, is an inspiring example of the die-hard spirit, although the author does not say so.

The city editor, Max Ways, turned young Mencken down cold on his first call, but he did say, vaguely, that he might call again at some future time. The young man was back the very next day and was waved away. "The third night," says Mencken, "Max simply shook his head, and so on the fourth, fifth, sixth, and seventh." On the eighth— "or maybe it was the ninth or tenth"—Mencken was told to come back, only to be turned away again, and thus it "went for four weeks, night in and night out." At last came the great day and Mencken's persistence was rewarded: Max Ways gave him his chance. A young man of less perseverance—*and of less imagination*—would have quit trying, and perhaps would have given up the newspaper business altogether. But Mencken *saw* himself in that job, and the picture gripped him and drove him on, relentlessly, to a great career in journalism.

Many businesses fall far short of their real potentials. When this happens you can be sure that either some necessary things are being done poorly or they are not being done at all. John Vivian found his idea in something not being done at all. The newspaper in his town, the *Golden Globe*, had never had a reporter. He laid siege to the editor, outlined just what he proposed: coverage of doings at the Court House, the Colorado School of Mines, the State Industrial School for Boys (all of them Golden institutions), and all social, business, and athletic events in general. John was only sixteen, but the editor bought the idea—for wages of two dollars and a half a week. Within three months circulation jumped and the unprofitable *Globe* began to make money—and has been making it ever since. Incidentally, in 1944 John C. Vivian was elected governor of Colorado.

Look at the businesses in your town. Which ones among them are doing necessary things poorly—or not at all? If there is a concern that interests you, take any job you can grab, get in on the insides watch the wheels go round. From this vantage point look sharp for better ways of doing things.

Yes, the job-getting anecdotes related here are a generation old. No matter. *Business, as always, is starved for ideas.* Every enterprise forever has problems—plenty of them. The competition ahead will be severe, and postwar products being developed in this new age of science will create thousands of jobs for young men of imagination. Did the tractor open up a new field for young fellows such as Edward Thye? So will television and radar and frozen foods and plastics and streamlined prefabricated houses. Freight by air stirs one's imagination. Today the business world will listen, as never before, to the man with an idea.

Make it a habit also to keep on the lookout for unusual ideas that others are already using successfully. Your idea needs to be original only in its application to your prospective employer's business. Watch the advertising in your local newspapers for new angles in store service. Study, too, the classified sections of the big telephone books. You will find many ads of specialized businesses with a novel twist, and you may have some talent or experience that fits right into one of these slots.

Every field of human activity is covered by America's 1,700 trade journals, whose business it is to report new ideas and developments. They're full of better ways of doing things. Employers and managers are often so busy they cannot search their trade magazines for ideas. The job-seeker who shows he has the energy to root them out, and the initiative to put them into practice, is certain to get an interested hearing.

The other day I asked a salesman for a big food house this question: "If you needed a job now, and the going was tough, what would you do?"

"I've been thinking about this," he replied, "and I've got it worked out. I'd go to some big outfit dealing in fish on the eastern seaboard, and I'd suggest they organize a '*Fish-of-the-month Club.*' Books and fruit are sold that way, and now I see they're selling phonograph records through a '*Music-of-the-month Club.*' Why not variety boxes of sea specialties like lobster, clams, pompano, crabs, and oysters? There are hundreds of inland towns that rarely get a taste of such delicacies. Deliveries could probably be made by refrigerator planes. I'd work out the idea on paper, with a scheme for mail-order advertising and all."

Maybe this young salesman's idea wouldn't work. But I am sure of this: his suggestion would be listened to with interest, and he would probably land a job because he had at least shown enough imagination to make a good try.

6
Limber Up Your Imagination

Hugo Münsterberg, the late and great Harvard psychologist, once wrote that even our most renowned thinkers seldom call into play more than a fraction of their true capacity for thought.

Millions of people travel from the cradle to the grave without thinking at all.

Every individual with a normal "head on his shoulders" and possessing normal energy, normal ambition, and normal curiosity, is *potentially* a thinker. The overwhelming tragedy is that so few people ever realize their potential—that so many, in fact, never come even close to it. They simply do not have the habit of thinking.

For I (Woolf) believe that the thinking habit can be cultivated. We are concerned in this book primarily with creative imagination: that, too, can be cultivated. For more than thirty years I worked in one of the toughest "idea professions" in the world—advertising. I was in charge of "creative production" for a big national advertising agency, which meant collaborating with a group of persons highly disciplined in the use of imagination. This experience convinces me that imagination is not a gift; it is a habitual way of using your mind.

Many times people have said to me, "I can't think up ideas. I guess I was born without imagination, and I go on doing the same old things in the same old way. My mind just doesn't seem to work creatively." Perhaps you have thus wondered at yourself. Usually the reason is—*habit*.

My answer to such confused individuals is always the same: "How hard do you try? Have you really made a determined effort over a long period of time to train yourself to think creatively?"

When as a young man I found a berth in the advertising agency just referred to, I am sure my imagination was very ordinary. One year in a small-town high school gave me little formal education, and in my former jobs as a railroad hand and a postal employee there is no record of my having contributed any ideas to the work. Why? Simply this, I think: ideas were not expected of me.

What followed convinces me that necessity is the mother not only of invention but also of imagination.

Ideas WERE expected of me by the agency: it was a case of imagination or—no job. I watched others around me to see how they did it. I discovered that creative thinking is—what shall I call it?—a sort of *trained* alertness, a *grooved* frame of mind, a *habitual* way of looking at things in search of ideas. It is a *developed* sensitivity to one's surroundings. Like the oldtime woods guide who trained his eyes to see on the trail portents invisible to the tenderfoot, the creative man drills himself in projecting his mind beyond the surface look of things. I do not believe those woodsmen were endowed with a special kind of sight; it was simply a case of had to—or else.

In my new job I presently found myself producing ideas almost instinctively. Looking at everything around me with a speculative eye became almost a normal pattern of behavior. Soon it was nearly impossible for me to see an article of merchandise without wondering, *automatically*, if it could be made better, packaged better, or sold and advertised in a better way.

Just as I made imaginative thinking my business—my daily work habit—so can you discipline yourself, force yourself into a routine of creative thinking every day of your life.

An Army Air Force colonel who, at the outset of the war, was given full responsibility for organizing and training a specialized unit for service in England, and who made a spectacular success of it, says this of his experience:

"My hardest job was that of teaching the boys the habit of original thinking. Most of them were from families in comfortable circumstances, and nearly all of them were college men. They were a bunch of grand lads—but I found, right at the start, that they had not developed the habit of thinking creatively for themselves. Why?

Simply because they never had had to think that way. It just wasn't a habit with them. At their homes, in their classrooms, at their summer camps, in nearly all of their supervised activities, a great part of their thinking had been done for them."

And then the colonel told me about Walter Fletcher (which is not his name) and how he changed from an old habit of doing little or no thinking—no real original thinking—to a new habit of using his head and using it hard.

"Walter," said the colonel, "would come to me with a rough draft of some proposal or other, and then, without showing the paper to me, would start baiting me with questions. It would be obvious that he had the glimmer of a new idea, but that he had not thought it through."

"'Walter,' I would say to him, 'it's pretty clear to me that you, perhaps unconsciously, are trying to get me to do your thinking for you. I think I have some of the ideas you are after, but I won't give them to you. You go back and dream them up for yourself—*and don't come back until you've got them.'*"

That kind of discipline, applied to yourself *by yourself*, will perform wonders.

But don't be too grim about it. Don't tighten up. Too much heavy concentration will stifle your imagination and give you a headache. New ideas will come from your ability to turn your mind loose, give it plenty of rope, let it play with fugitive thoughts even if apparently they have no immediate relation to your problem. It is a mistake, in your eagerness to focus on your original notion, to cast aside what may seem at first to be irrelevant or even silly ideas. Did not Charles Darwin often play with what he called "Fool's Experiments"?

Don't lose sight of your objective, of course, but concentrate only to the extent of keeping your thoughts moving toward your desired end.

"Nearly all creative men," Woodrow Wilson once said, "are dreamers." Emerson's daily routine provided time for "meditating quietly before brooks."

But grim bulldog concentration isn't meditation. Quite the reverse. So close your eyes and dream, explore the back rooms of

your mind for memories—for it is memories of what you knew yesterday compounded with what you know today that produce fresh
ideas. Recollection of a long succession of small experiences, old
and new, is the stuff imagination is made of. Such recollection is
throttled when your mind, "grooved" by fevered concentration on
a single notion or concept, lacks freedom of movement and spon-
taneity. Professor William James reports that a friend of his, when
in pursuit of a desired idea, was always helped by letting his mind
"wander in random directions."

Free and fertile play of the imagination—not the kinked and
furrowed brow, not the taut pose of Rodin's "Thinker"—is the outstanding characteristic of the truly creative brain. Relax. Keep your
mind open. Edison, when asked if he sat down and thought things
out, replied: "No, not always. Often they just happen. I start here
with the intention of reaching here (Edison was tracing with his
finger) in an experiment, say, to increase the speed of the Atlantic
Cable; but when I arrive part way in my straight line, I meet with a
phenomenon and it leads me off in another direction and develops
into a phonograph."

Often you will find it helps to pick up a pencil and play with
words. "Thought engenders thought. Place one idea on paper, another will follow it, and still another, until you have written a page;
you cannot fathom your mind. There is a well of thought there
which has no bottom; the more you draw from it, the more clear
and fruitful it will be." This is not a new technique. George Augus-
tus Sala, once a great English war correspondent, wrote that nearly
a hundred years ago.

There is this plus-advantage to the pencil-and-paper method.
If you catch yourself writing down the same word or thought over
and over again, you'll see that your mind has a fixation and is whirl-
ing around hopelessly in a tight little circle. This is the time to
loosen up and start writing down anything that comes into your
head.

A student of Dr. Frank L. Tibolt, well-known psychologist, said
to him, "I'm just a dumb farmer and I guess I don't belong in your
class. My mind seems to be blacked out and my brain cells are on a
sit-down strike. I just can't think up new ideas."

"What," asked Dr. Tibolt, "is your most pressing immediate problem?"

"Selling more eggs," the young farmer replied.

"I told him," relates Dr. Tibolt, "that he was thinking too hard about selling eggs. I advised him to go home and to spend fifteen minutes every day writing down all the words he could think of, not merely words about eggs, but about people and life and things in general. He wrote earnestly for several days, wrote page after page of words, arriving finally at a word he saw on a passing bread truck: *vitamins*. Here, it finally turned out, was his idea! Not a new word, of course, but somehow he hadn't thought of it before. The next week he came to my class and read a folder he got up advertising eggs with extra vitamin D from irradiated hens. This idea has so far increased his sales 30%. And all because his pencil got him off a single track of thinking."

This method, however, must not be permitted to let the thinker hibernate from the world around him. Time and again in my advertising work, in search of a novel twist, a fresh approach, a new "angle," I would find my mind worrying a single notion as a dog does a bone. A sort of hypnosis would shackle my imagination. Then (I've done it countless times) I would quit concentrating and go "shopping" to break my spell. I would stroll along Chicago's Michigan Avenue or State Street, idle before its exciting windows, wander up and down the glittering aisles in the stores, looking and listening. Or maybe I would see an art exhibit, a movie, or play a game of golf.

Once a shoe manufacturer, a client of my agency, wanted a new promotion idea for his retailers. After a couple of days of futile concentration, I went "shopping." I listened to some records in a music store, saw a style show in a department store, heard a Paris designer in a dress shop talk about the new styles.

My client's shoe stores were situated mostly in small cities and towns. "Why," I wondered, "can't these little stores put on a fancy style show, too?" Well, the idea turned out to be a fine success. Each store was provided with a manual on "How to Stage a Style Show" (music, models, flowers for the ladies, and so on), and also with a speech by a "fashion authority"—a phonograph recording of a specially written talk by a Paris designer, accent and all. That idea didn't come from "concentration."

A man I know, a business friend, combines the "play-with-words" technique with the "shopping" technique of observation. He carries with him always a packet of two- by four-inch blank cards, using them for jotting down "association words" when he sees or hears something that might have some bearing, however remote, on whatever problem he is working on. Not long ago, interested in luminous plastics, he was eager to find a new use for them. Glow-in-the-dark house numbers, fishing bait, doorknobs, and signs were common enough. For several days as he went about his business—in his home, his office, his factory, on the streets—he jotted down words and phrases on his little cards: *cellar, attic, closet, garage, automobile, scooter, bicycle, dark, night, rain, water, bathroom, bedroom, bed, bedside table, bedside drinking glass*—ah! he had it! A tumbler holder that could be seen in the dark. Wasn't his wife forever knocking over her nighttime glass of water! My friend is now completing plans to add this new product to his already popular line of household merchandise.

The dangers inherent in becoming obsessed by a single idea or mental attitude is recognized by Otto F. Reiss (*How to Develop Profitable Ideas*), brilliant advertising man. When you are looking for a new idea, he advises that you prepare what he calls a "hunch list"—jot down from thirty to fifty ideas, however random and fragmentary, even if they are outside of your immediate problem. But don't get brainfag over it. After a good try, put your hunch list away and go for a walk. Next day put a check mark in front of the jottings that seem to have at least a kernel of an idea.

Don't be too intent, Reiss says, on a deathless idea. Climb down a step or two in your aspirations. If it isn't a major invention, you can make it a toy. For example, an automobile that, like a horse, obeys the voice of its owner, would be a spectacular idea indeed. The problem is far from a practical solution. But the man who had the idea, and used it in a toy—a miniature car controlled by the sound of a whistle—made a lot of money.

It is well to bear in mind that there is probably no such thing as a completely new idea. What you seek to do is to reassemble and rearrange old ideas into new combinations. Says Edward Wortley, "One of the most fruitful methods of getting original ideas is that of taking some principle now in use in one or more connections and extending its application, that is to say, applying it to new uses." (*How to Get Original Ideas.*) He gives as a striking example of originality produced by analogical thinking the invention of the Schick Injector Razor. The particular advantage of this improved shaving implement lies in the fact that in loading and unloading it the blade does not come in contact with the hand. The new blades, protected and sealed in a bath of oil, are contained in a magazine attached (for loading purposes) to the razor. The magazine itself has an injector, and by a simple pull and push on this the old blade is ejected automatically from the razor and a new one is injected. This action is said to have been based upon the principle of the repeating rifle, and it is of interest to note that the inventor of the Schick Injector Razor had been an army man.

What goes for mechanical invention also goes for the creating of business-building plans and ideas. I have before me a letter from Bernard A. Mayer, an ex-serviceman, which illustrates the point. Mr. Mayer has started a new business which is attracting wide attention and promises to go places in a big way. He conceived—and operates—the "Frostmobile," a mobile frosted-foods store. His letter says that, back from the war, he bought a bus from a transit company in Washington, D.C., had all the seats removed, and installed frozen-food cabinets of the same kind now used in grocery stores. The driver of the Frostmobile pulls up to an area, blows a musical horn to let the housewife know that he is in that particular area, and then awaits the arrival of the customers, who come a few minutes later. The customer enters by the rear door, picks out her commodities, pays the driver, and exits by the front door.

"This idea," says Mr. Mayer, "is brand new." Well, it is—and it isn't. It is simply a blend of old ideas mixed together in an appetizing new concoction. For centuries mobile vehicles have peddled foods from house to house. Frosted foods themselves are no longer new and neither are frozen-food cabinets. And as far back as 1937, open trucks peddled frosted foods much after the manner of the Frostmobile, but the scheme failed in winter largely because the housewife refused to stand outside and be frozen herself while she was buying frozen foods. To these old ingredients Mayer adds one inviting new touch—the idea of having the housewife do her shopping *inside* the enclosed and comfortable Frostmobile.

H. A. Overstreet puts it this way: "In its passive role, the mind collects experiences. In its active role, it reconstructs experiences. Both are necessary." (*Let Me Think.*) Mayer's mind, in its passive role, made a number of observations with reference to frosted foods and methods of selling them—idle observations, perhaps, and with no intention at the time for making later use of them. Back from the war, seeking a business opportunity, his mind reconstructed those observations, fitted them together (synthesis), and up popped a new idea—the Frostmobile.

No mind can produce ideas—think creatively—if it fails in its role of collecting experiences. Marshall Field, the founder of Chicago's celebrated department store, made it a practice to stroll every day up and down the aisles of his store and eavesdrop on conversations between customers and clerks. In this way his imagination was stimulated to formulate the policies that made his business so successful. He was quick, too, to observe what other stores were doing and to adapt the new ideas of others in the solution of his own problems. Says Overstreet further: "Without the gathering of experience, our actions would be careless and probably mistaken. Without the reconstruction of experience, nothing would be changed from what it is now to what we should rather have it be. There would be stones, but no stone walls; forests, but no orchards; sounds, but no music."

The collecting of experiences, however, ceases to be a passive role when you consciously set out to apply your mind to a specific and immediate problem. Now you apply your active mind to gathering new experiences—and all the information you can find—anything that bears on the matter in hand. Your chances of producing a worth-while idea are immeasurably increased if your mind is saturated with a knowledge of your subject. A clear understanding of your objective and a thorough study of all the information pertaining to it are essential to finding the answers you seek. This fact-finding approach to problem solving and idea production is definitely a matter of discipline. You can school yourself in this procedure as an instinctive and automatic routine.

Has sales volume in the children's department of your store gone down dangerously? Why? Is your competition underpricing you? Are you slow in stocking the newest and most up-to-date merchandise? Are the salespeople in the department lazy, discourteous, unskilled in salesmanship? Is the manager of the department too conservative, unprogressive, behind the times? Is the department badly situated in the store, perhaps on the wrong floor? What new things are your competitors doing? Is children's business drifting away from department stores and going to specialty shops? These questions—and many more—should be studied as the first step in the production of ideas you are looking for to solve your problem.

All right—now you have all your facts and you know them so well that you can recite them upside down and downside up. What next? Well, what you do next is to lock them up in your desk; throw away your key, and try to forget them. To sit and glare at a mess of charts and graphs and tables of statistics will smother your imagination and give you an awful headache. Remember, as has already been stated, that new ideas come from the ability to turn your mind loose, give it plenty of rope, let it play with fugitive thoughts and "wander in random directions." I am especially intrigued by Mr. Beardsley Ruml's procedure. "Ruml's method of tackling problems," reports the *New Yorker*, "is to sit in a chair and do nothing. He had advised executives who have problems on their hands to lock themselves up, sit in a chair, and do nothing for at least an hour a day. It is essential for apprentices at musing and daydreaming that there be no newspapers or other reading matter around to break the spell." And no graphs and charts and tables of statistics!

Never, never fool yourself with the notion that you are thinking creatively when you read up on a new problem or undertaking. A friend whom I shall call Edward Wilkerson set himself up, some years back, in the investment brokerage business. He had considerable capital for the financing of his enterprise, but almost no practical experience and no ideas. He thereupon launched himself on a program of fact gathering: he read dozens of books, beginning with Adam Smith, on the philosophy of money. He had long talks with successful bankers and brokers and he filed away in his brain their opinions and prejudices. He subscribed to the important financial trade journals and for weeks he read them from cover to cover.

Unfortunately, he confused *reading* (fact finding) with creative thinking. He collected hundreds of facts, but he failed to see them in relation to one another, failed to generalize them into a few clear-cut fundamental truths. His reading provided him with so many ready-made answers that he had no real ideas and convictions—the products of original thought—on how to operate his business; and consequently he failed.

Summing up, it boils down to this: *You can discipline yourself deliberately to be a creative thinker.* You can make ideas your hobby. Each day, when you awake to a new sunrise, you can train yourself to open your eyes wide to the ever challenging world around you. You can teach yourself to take a fresh and curious look at everything that falls under your gaze, at even the little things in the ordinary routine of your everyday life. You can make it a habit to say to yourself every morning, as you hang up your hat in your store, your office, your shop, your factory: "Surely, there must be better ways of doing things around here! Now let me see. . . ."

Practice at it all the time. Limber up, limber up, limber up. Do you drive your car along the same humdrum route every morning as you go to work? What do you see? What do you think about? Have you ever tried asking yourself questions like these:

How can that morning traffic jam at Walnut and Market be avoided? Why are there so many accidents where Walnut crosses Highway 85? How can that icy stretch on Elm Street be made safer in winter? Maybe such questions have nothing to do with your business, but they are mighty good exercises for limbering your imagination.

And tonight, after you settle yourself snugly in your easy chair, try taking a fresh look at what goes on around you.

Is everything as it should be? Listen to that faucet which has been dripping off and on for months. *Must* faucets be that way? Listen to Alice fussing at that refrigerator. *Must* ice cubes always stick? And those cold, wet milk bottles that slip so disastrously from one's fingers? *Must* they? How would you make them? Let's see now. Do you suppose that if the necks of the bottles were ridged like corrugated cardboard . . . ?

It's really pretty simple. Originality has been defined as a pair of fresh eyes. Overstreet once wrote, "A man and his mind go forth together every morning." And to the extent that his eyes are fresh and his mind curious will he be unwilling to accept his faulty world as it is, and something in his life is going to be different.

7
SEE WITH THE OTHER FELLOW'S EYES

Four brothers in Illinois were left, by their father, a business that had more liabilities than assets. It was broke. The reason it had descended to this state was that strong competition in the form of chain stores had entered the town. The founder of the business just hadn't been able to meet the competition.

The elder of the brothers called the other three together and told them, "It's a cinch we won't have much of a chance unless we can make the people of the town and surrounding country like us. That's our only hope, to develop such friendliness that people will want to trade with us."

He was, don't you see, applying his imagination to a specific problem. It takes imagination always to project yourself into the other fellow's shoes, to see what he wants, then to give it to him.

No form of imagination you can use will pay you greater dividends than the one this brother proposed should be applied in rejuvenating the business—the form of imagination that consists of seeing things through the other fellow's eyes, adjusting your desires to his, giving him what he wants of you and your services.

This is not only an important phase of imagination: it is also a difficult one. The reason why it is difficult is that all of us all our lives look inward—at ourselves—rather than outward—at others. From infancy we are dominated by our egos. We use the personal pronoun *I* five times as much as we use the word *you*. We don't, you can see, use imagination as much as we should in dealing with others.

But let us get on with the story of the four brothers and their imaginative approach to their problem. It's a success story with imagination playing the title role. For by seeing everything from the customer's point of view, by doing things they knew would please the customer, by being extremely friendly and personal with everyone who came into the store, it didn't take the brothers long to capture their market. Competition simply had no chance in the face of this friendly, imaginative attack.

Not only did the brothers succeed in reestablishing their business to former size and importance but they carried it a step further. Soon they had the largest store in the county. Not too long afterward they had the largest store in the state. The business is still thriving—on imagination.

The case of the four brothers and their business has been cited to show you that if you want to get along better with others, you don't have another aid in your life that can be compared with imagination. I should like to give you a few suggestions (based upon the lives of men and women who used imagination in attaining their success) that I (Roth) believe will help you in your contacts with others every day.

Suppose we start with the key subject of the brothers in the story I just told you—friendliness.

Some persons seem to have a genius for making friends. Some do not. William Hazlitt, a fine writer, declares that there is only one class of persons who cannot make friends. Who are the members of this class?

"They're folks who can't *be* friends. They have no interest in other people, exhibit no traits of friendliness toward them. They're selfish. They think only of their own affairs. They are intent only on their own thoughts."

Now, those who make friends are just the opposite: they think of others first, of themselves second. They attract friends merely by being so friendly that it is impossible not to be friendly with them. They have, whether they express it overtly or not, the same philosophy that Will Rogers had. He said, you will remember, "I never met a man I didn't like." And that is the philosophy—the imaginative philosophy—of a man who had a million friends because he was the friend of a million people!

Another place where imagination helps you in getting along better with others is in showing you how futile is the common practice of finding fault. It's perfectly natural (that's the ego working again, you see) for you, if you feel you are right, to pick flaws in other persons—to find fault. Yet if you want to get along better with others, to see with the other fellow's eyes, you won't find fault at all. What will you do? You will praise instead.

It's better not to criticize anyone for anything he does, but I know and you know that occasionally criticism is necessary, because people do need to be corrected. Does it mean you have to lose their good will when you have to correct others? Not at all. If you correct people in the right way you can still keep their friendship and good will—but the right way entails the use of a little imagination.

Recently in addressing a small private group, Dale Carnegie outlined some good rules for correcting others and keeping their friendship and respect.

These are the Carnegie rules:

1. Wait twenty-four hours, if possible, before you correct the person. Don't correct him while you're still angry or before you have had a chance to think the situation through. Wait a while.

2. Never correct a person in the presence of anyone else. This embarrasses him. An embarrassed person is seldom friendly.

3. Before you correct a person find something about him or what he has done to praise, so as to take the "edge" off your criticism.

4. Instead of attacking the person head-on, inquire as to the reason for his making the mistake you wish to correct. In other words, try to get his viewpoint before correcting him.

5. Be as moderate as you can in your criticism.

Whenever it becomes necessary for you to criticize someone, keep in mind this moderate method. Good will is its result; ill will is the result of another method—one that doesn't take into consideration the place of imagination even in correcting the mistakes of others.

To show you how an imaginative man handles delicate situations between individuals, I want to retell an incident in the life of Benjamin Franklin. As a young man, in Philadelphia, he incurred the wrath of one of the city's most influential men, an old Quaker who was given to holding grudges.

After several months of ill feeling between them, Franklin decided that it was to his advantage to win the enemy's friendship. With the lively imagination that characterized his entire career, he worked out a technique which is still used every day by successful men and women. Instead of apologizing, demeaning himself, or ignoring the enemy, what did Franklin do? He did the imaginative thing: he asked the enemy to do him, Franklin, a favor. The favor he asked was that he be permitted to read a certain book—one that the old Quaker was proud of.

You can see what this shrewd piece of human engineering did, can't you? It appealed to the other man's ego. He was glad to grant the favor because it gave him such a big buildup to be important to another man. He lent Franklin the book—and with this gesture he yielded his complete confidence and friendship.

Two businessmen I know had a quarrel over some sort of deal they had engaged in together. They bitterly opposed each other, and these bad feelings continued for several years. Eventually it was to the advantage of one of these men then to win the other to his side. How could he make the advances without belittling himself or running the risk of being turned down?

He used the Franklin technique. He wrote a brief note asking the other man to do him a slight favor of a personal kind. That brought the miffed executive in person to his erstwhile enemy, apologizing for his rash action in being and remaining angry—and granting the favor.

Behind this simple act of asking another person to do you a favor is a sound principle in handling people.

Most persons feel more friendly toward you after they have performed some slight favor, provided, naturally, that performing this favor affords them satisfaction, increases their self-esteem. Back of that feeling of theirs is the ego. When you ask a person to do you some slight favor, you appeal to his ego. And the leaders of mankind all use the egos of those around them every day of their lives.

I think that you have been able to tell from the few examples I have given you thus far that seeing life through the other fellow's eyes requires the constant use of imagination. It is much easier to see life through your own eyes; so much easier, indeed, that most persons never take the trouble of seeing it through any other eyes but their own. But the leaders do. They know that if you want to win others, to influence others, to make them like you, you must see through their eyes.

Take so simple a matter as courtesy. I term courtesy a simple matter, and it is. But it is also an extremely important matter, because courtesy is another of those keys to open the hearts of everyone around you. Yet what is courtesy but treating others as you would like to be treated?

A writer named Jonathan Johns recently entered the offices of a large corporation in New York—but let him tell what happened.

"As I was escorted from doorman to vice-president by office boys and ushers, I felt my spirits rising. By the time I reached the vice-president's office, I felt as if I were a prince or a potentate of some kind. The happy courtesy with which I was treated all the way was the cause of it.

"When I mentioned it to an employee later, he replied, 'That is one reason why this organization has grown so rapidly. The founder would never employ a brusque or ill-mannered person. He insists that we be a little more courteous than anyone else.

"'What dividends this has paid! It prevents internal friction; cushions our contact with the public, and makes friends for us, thus building an invaluable amount of good will.'"

The chances are that this same force of courtesy, if you were to use your imagination to see how you could use it more and more each day, would do just as much for you as it did for that New York corporation. You can prove this easily enough, if you want to. Just go on a courtesy basis for one day—say, tomorrow. See if you don't have more influence on others and get more out of your day's living yourself than you ever did before. Try that.

Another thing which imaginative men and women do in dealing with others is to make everything extremely clear, so as to be understood perfectly.

A New York newspaper editor not long ago sent one of his reporters to ascertain, if he could, the chief characteristic of successful men and women.

The reporter interviewed over a hundred eminently successful and accomplished persons, and reached this conclusion: that while a successful person has to have other attributes, one of the chief reasons for success is that of making himself clear to the other person.

In the make-up of these successful men and women there was no double talk, no cloudy statements, no long words, no involved syntax. They made everything clear. Because they did this they were understood. Because they were understood they were believed.

In a day when speakers were given to hyperbole and bombast, Wendell Phillips went about the country talking in crystal-clear phrases—and winning confidence and support.

In a day when writers were wont to use two long words where one short word would do, Macaulay wrote a history which even a child could understand—and became the most popular writer of his day.

Anyone who wishes to win the friendship and confidence of others can do no better than to follow the plan of Wendell Phillips and T. B. Macaulay and those hundred successful New Yorkers—make sure he is understood.

Next to clarity in influencing and impressing others favorably comes brevity. If you once get the reputation for being a "long-story" man or woman, you will be avoided, not welcomed. One man talks so long and so tiresomely that whenever he calls, I can always manage to find an excuse for not seeing him. Yet some of the things he wants to tell me I should like very much to hear. I am willing to forego any profit that might come from a talk with him for the sake of being spared his long discourses.

"The best salesman uses as few words as possible," says a writer. "The long-winded talker is tiresome, and often talks himself out of a sale. Who explains and defends his cause too volubly, proclaims a weak case. A good one needs little recommendation.

"At Gettysburg, Lincoln said more in three minutes than his predecessor on the speaker's platform did in two hours. The short speech was a masterpiece; the long one is forgotten.

"The shrewd preacher realizes that few souls are saved after the first twenty minutes of his sermon. The visitor who does not wear out his welcome gets another invitation."

Like most arts, that of brevity has to be acquired.

It is acquired by paying attention to yourself when you speak. Are you reducing what you want to say to an absolute minimum? Is there a quicker, an easier, a more interesting way to say it?

A good practice, when you have something important to say and want to pare it down to its essentials, is to write out the material first.

The best talkers, as a matter of fact, are often brief to the point of being silent; their art is in getting the other man to talk, you see. While he talks, they listen, and in listening pick up cues for handling him. In addition, they pick up mines of valuable information.

If you will apply enough imagination to your contacts with others to realize that if you will keep still and encourage the other person to talk, you will win the reputation for being a good conversationalist, and an interesting person to be around. And that sort of reputation, of course, will help you no matter what you are trying to do.

There is one other place where imagination certainly enters into the subject of getting along with others. It is in sizing people up and judging whether you are going to like or dislike them on the basis of your conclusion.

Since the beginning of time, men have sought an infallible system for judging others. But no system is as effective as a simple program of procedure which was explained several years ago by the late Dr. Frank Crane.

"In preparing to judge others, the main thing is to look inside ourselves," Dr. Crane declared, "since most of our errors come from our own defects.

"The best judge of all is liking other people. If you detest a person, if you feel an instinctive antipathy, do not undertake to form any opinion of him. You are pretty certain to be wrong.

"Second, you must be honest. If you are crafty, devious, and unfair, you can never know the truth. No man can see the honesty in another unless he has it in himself.

"Third, you must strip yourself of pride, egotism, and the sensitiveness that goes with these failings. If you are touchy in your self-esteem, you cannot see other souls, but only the shadow of your own.

"Finally, you must be open-minded. You must be able to keep your judgment suspended. Then you must have imagination, for without that you cannot put yourself in the other person's place—and if you cannot put yourself in his place, you cannot understand him."

To please others in little things is another secret of handling others, and that, of course, requires about as much imagination as anything can. Business has come to realize of late years that only by getting the customer's point of view and serving him from that point of view can a business thrive.

Unless you are familiar with the practice of business in seeking the customer's point of view, you would be astonished at the lengths to which business goes in studying the customer and trying to see through his (the other fellow's) eyes.

The name of this practice is "consumer opinion survey," and organizations like the United States Steel Corporation and General Motors maintain large and expensive departments for the sake of getting down and finding out what their customers want.

This is applying imagination in the most practical way in the world: find out what people want, then give it to them. In your own life you should use the same technique. What, for instance, do others want in you, as an employee, or as a businessman, as a salesman, or as a friend? Find that out, then custom-make your personality and demeanor to them, and you cannot help but win success.

One of the outstanding businessmen of a few years ago was a man named Ralph Hitz, a hotel manager who was given the job of building the business for the largest hotel in New York City, at that time a pretty sick elephant.

What did Ralph Hitz do first? He found out what guests wanted in a hotel, down to the kind of soap they preferred for their bath. He spent months studying people, what they liked, what they disliked. When he began giving them what they wanted in hotel service, his business skyrocketed, and his hotel became the most successful of all time.

What did Ralph Hitz discover his guests wanted above all else? The feeling of personal importance! They all wanted to be big shots, recognized by elevator pilots, bellboys, and headwaiters. They wanted to be called by name. They wanted to have their little whims and wishes gratified. And when one man was intelligent enough to see through the guests' eyes, they rewarded him handsomely.

His specific methods are examples of imagination in practical form. When you registered at the hotel, the clerk, in calling a bell-boy to carry your luggage, purposely spoke your name in a loud enough tone of voice for the bellboy to hear. "Take Mr. Andrews to Room 413," he would say. As he put you on the elevator, the bell-boy would repeat the procedure, speaking your name loud enough for the elevator pilot to hear. "Right this way, Mr. Andrews," the bellboy said. When the pilot stopped the car on the fourth floor, she would say, "This is your floor, Mr. Andrews." And so it went, with everyone in the hotel calling Mr. Andrews by name, until he was quite certain that although he wasn't appreciated at home, here in New York, where it meant something to be important, he was indeed a big, big man. Do you think Mr. Andrews would go to another hotel the next time he went to New York City?

The ability to understand people from their point of view and to please them is so important in getting ahead and in winning friends that psychologists today give all knowledge and skill in that field a distinct name. They call it "social intelligence." The other form of intelligence they call "abstract intelligence."

Social intelligence is intelligence of human beings, while abstract intelligence is intelligence of things. Many a person has high abstract intelligence, low social intelligence. For all their learning, such men and women are seldom as successful as they should be, because the fact is that social intelligence, even in highly technical occupations like accounting and engineering and surgery, is fully as important as abstract intelligence.

A brilliant young woman I know, working in a large office, was discouraged over the slow progress she was making. She was intelligent (had abstract intelligence, that is), had good training, but she didn't seem to have the knack of handling others, of understanding them, of getting along with them. She was handicapped, and knew it.

She went one day to the firm's vice-president, who happens to be one of my friends and is a wise man, and told him her trouble. Used by long years of experience to sizing up others and spotting their difficulties, the vice-president, when he had heard the young woman's plight, suggested she begin a three-way program to improve her social intelligence.

He told her to:

Increase her recreational habits—learn to do more things with more people—play bridge, golf, tennis, and swim. These things lead to better adjustment to others—give you a chance to see things with the other fellow's eyes, you know.

Take a greater interest in others. Like most girls who did not find the world completely to her liking, this young woman had put into her life too many introverted thoughts. Her boss suggested she call someone at least three times a week for lunch, and spend more time with others.

Study how to influence others. This was his third suggestion, that she learn the fine human art of keeping step with others, of understanding them. Included in this were the arts of complimenting others, listening while they talk, and pleasing them.

What he was trying to tell this girl to do is what I have been telling you to do in this chapter from my first word—use your imagination to see through the other person's eyes.

Did it work out in her case? Beautifully. Not long afterward her chief called the girl into his office and told her she was being promoted to a position with an executive title. This, her chief told me, was almost entirely the result of her having acquired more social intelligence.

Business has always rewarded those with social intelligence, because business depends upon knowledge of people fully as much as it does upon knowledge of things, and any man or woman who will become more versed in doing and saying what will please others will be given greater responsibilities and will earn more money.

To me the fascinating thing about using one's imagination to see the world through the other fellow's eyes is that it does lead to such vast rewards—not only the material rewards of more money, which everyone covets, but also to other rewards equally important. The rewards I have in mind are more friendships, more interesting hours with others, and the satisfaction that can come only to those who see eye to eye with other human beings and live with them in peace and comity, not at cross-purposes and therefore with dissatisfaction.

8
A Million Ideas Die A-borning

In discussing the failure of a business to which he had given thirty years of his life and his complete attention, a friend of mine (Roth) named George S. Clason, now happily reestablished in another business, which he likes better than he did his first, told me it wasn't any lack of ideas which brought him to disaster.

"My business never suffered from a shortage of ideas," is the way he put it. "No, sir. As a matter of fact, we always had more ideas than we could use. No idea shortage caused our trouble."

"What did, then?"

"Our failure to put ideas to work. You see, having imagination, ideas, is only half the battle. The other half is using your ideas."

"I see."

"The big lesson I learned out of failure," declared Mr. Clason, "was that it's better to have just one idea and put it to work full time, than to have half a dozen different ideas—and do nothing about them."

I said I was beginning to see what he was driving at, and George Clason continued.

"One of the things I resolved when I started my new business was that whenever I had an idea, I would study it for workability. If it had the slightest chance of being put to work, I followed it through—to the very end. If, on the other hand, it was a mere daydream, I would chase it from my mind."

"Did that system work better?" I asked.

Mr. Clason's subsequent success gave me my answer. Starting at an age when many persons would tell you that reestablishing yourself in business is impossible, he has built a business which is enviably large and profitable.

The history of business is filled with stories of men with imagination and good ideas who did nothing about them. Dr. Donald F. Laird, for instance, says that he knew a man who discovered wireless ten years before Marconi got around to it. This man, a genius in invention, worked out the principle of radio, tested it, conducted experiments for several years. That he had the right principle there was not the slightest doubt.

But he did nothing about it. He had the idea, fine. But there the matter rested—it was only an idea, a proved idea. A decade later came Marconi. He went through the same experiments, made the same discovery. But he was a man who acted upon his ideas. He did something about his discovery, put it to practical use. The result was radio for the world—and a *twenty-million-dollar* fortune for Marconi.

Another man had imagination and ideas that could have died a-borning but for the influence on his life of his wife. He was Leo Tolstoy, the greatest of Russian writers. Always a dreamer—that is to say, a man with imagination, ideas—Tolstoy as a mere boy saw the need for someone who would help elevate and improve the lot of the Russian peasant. They suffered bitterly under oppression, and no one lifted his voice in their behalf. Tolstoy saw the time when the Russians would be given a fair chance at life. That was his big idea. And it became an obsession with him. But there he was content to rest: he did nothing about putting his idea into action.

The chances are he might have drifted throughout his life, carrying that burning idea in his mind yet doing nothing to put it into practice. When he was thirty-four he married an alert, intelligent woman. To her he naturally confided his big idea.

She saw the point.

"It's a fine idea," she agreed. "But what are you doing about it?"

"Nothing."

"Nothing? Why not? If the idea is sound, if the reforms are needed, why don't you do something about it yourself?"

The result of the Countess Tolstoy's insistence that ideas must be lived as well as thought was that Tolstoy started writing his great social novels. These certainly contributed something to the Russian peasant, and to the world as well. But if it hadn't been for the intervention of this practical-minded woman, Tolstoy might never have been heard of outside his little circle in Russia.

Ask any businessman who has had much to do with ideas that are brought to him what he thinks the greatest mistake of those with ideas is. He will probably tell you that there are two mistakes. The first is that those who have ideas do not think their ideas through clearly enough before they try to tell them to someone else. The second mistake is that very few persons who have ideas have a clear-cut plan for carrying their ideas out.

One of my friends, Douglas E. Lurton, the noted and successful editor of several self-help magazines, has no patience with what he calls "the usual crop of half-baked ideas" that cross his desk in the course of the year.

"I have had my fill of boys and girls who have half-baked ideas they are sure are good, but that they haven't worked out sufficiently to know whether they are good or not," he wrote me not long ago.

"Some of the chief failures of the boys and girls who figure they are presenting bright ideas that others are too dumb to accept is due to the fact that they do not present their ideas *clearly*. You and I have seen that on innumerable occasions, I am sure. I have seen the thing with new ideas for new magazines. For instance, I have created several magazines as well as those now in our set-up, and have always been able to present my ideas for them in a few words and without a dummy. But I find publishers here in New York who are utterly incapable of grasping the idea for a new magazine, and the only way they can be interested is to stick their noses into a complete dummy. They simply can't visualize the possibilities otherwise."

As to their wanting someone else to carry them out, Mr. Lurton has much to say. In most cases where the idea is not accepted, he believes, it's because the person who submitted the idea doesn't have sufficient faith in it to back it up himself.

Says Mr. Lurton, "The attitude of most persons is that of, 'Why don't you get somebody to do this?' instead of, 'I'm ready to go ahead on this.' The thing I am looking for in a man with ideas is, first, one who will think his idea out so clearly that he is willing to accept the full responsibility for carrying it out, and, second, a desire on his part to carry out his idea to the very end.

"When I meet a man who combines these two qualities with the ideas he submits to me, I know that I am talking to a man whose ideas have a chance of becoming successful realities."

Of course, the reason why you find so little follow-through on ideas is that having ideas is easier than putting those ideas into working clothes. That entails work. It entails attention. It entails constant application. It also involves disappointment: many new ideas have to struggle hard for existence.

There is, however, another reason why many persons with ideas let them die a-borning. It is that they cannot stand having their cherished ideas criticized. When you think of it that's silly. The fact is that some of the best ideas, ideas which resulted in fame, fortune, satisfaction to their originators, had to undergo years of criticism and many revisions before they actually were in a form to be of practical use. Maybe you remember reading about how Robert Fulton was ridiculed for his idea of a steamship. "Fulton's Folly" they called his idea. And even Henry Ford's father thought his boy profoundly stupid to give up a $125-a-month job with the power company to fiddle with a horseless carriage.

Fairly typical of the attitude of the majority of men and women toward their ideas when criticism comes along is that of a youngster I helped put into business not long ago. Having helped him get started—and being interested in him because he has been a family friend for so long—I naturally was eager to see him make good. I wanted to help. One day I talked to one of his clients, asked about the service the boy was rendering. I discovered that, from the customer's point of view, there was a serious lack in what he was offering. I called this fact to the attention of my young friend.

Instead of accepting the criticism and benefiting by it, what did he do but take umbrage, flare up, and upbraid me!

"Nobody can find fault with my ideas," said he, testily. "I can work out all the things you have told me about, without the help of anybody."

So I left him to work out all those things without the help of anybody, but I shook my head sadly, because he is so far wrong in his attitude. The fact is that all business is based upon getting the customer's point of view—and then carrying out that point of view in the way the customer wants it carried out.

And this applies to ideas. If your ideas are criticized, if you have to change them all around, alter them to suit your market, do it gladly, do it gratefully, for an idea is of value only when it is accepted by someone else and put to work.

Everything I have told you thus far in urging you to put your ideas into use is described by one word. That word is *initiative*.

You know, of course, the meaning of initiative. It is to initiate—to put into action. And if you want to make the most of your imagination, of your ideas, you must initiate them—put them into action so that they will become deeds, not words; results, not mere promises.

Whenever you find a man or a woman who recognizes the extreme importance of imagination and ideas, who consciously learns the technique of creating ideas and practices having ideas all the time—and then on top of that does something about putting those ideas into action just as quickly as possible, you have the successful man or woman.

In other words, *imagination plus initiative is the winning combination.*

Let me give you an example of what initiative—and also lack of initiative—will do. Ten years ago one of my clients asked me to help him pick out two youngsters for his company's sales force from the graduates of a leading university of commerce.

After careful consideration we picked our two. Both, I am glad to report, have made good, because both had and still have imagination, ideas. But one of these boys has done ever so much better than the other. Today he is his boss's assistant, and if he misses becoming a vice-president by the time he's forty, I'll be badly disillusioned about my ability as a prophet. The other boy is still on

the job as a line salesman, getting by, you understand, but not setting the river afire.

Yet between the two men when we hired them there didn't appear to be a hair of difference. They were the same age, the same
size, had the same educational background—and both had ideas.
That was the deciding factor in their selection in the first place—
their imagination. Yet one man has far outstripped the other. Why?

The other day I asked their boss that question. He had been
thinking about the matter himself, because he had the answer on
the tip of his tongue.

"It's easy," said he. "Max has initiative. Harry waits for somebody to tell him what to do when he has an idea."

There you have it.

Because I consider this matter of initiative so important, I want
you to consider the word and its meaning with me for a little while.
The dictionary defines initiative as "the power of initiating, the
ability for original conception and independent action." More practical than the dictionary's definition of the word is that of Elbert
Hubbard. Initiative is merely "doing the right thing without being
told," said he—and added, "The world bestows its big prizes both
in money and in honor but for one thing. That is initiative."

Please note the phrase "the right thing" in the Hubbard definition. That's the crux of this whole matter. The world is filled with
men and women who "buzz around" like so many bees, filling their
days from morning till night with incessant activity—and always
doing the wrong thing. Such men and women reap little reward,
often no reward.

One of the most active men I have ever known has worked all
his life at least sixteen hours a day. He never takes time out to
loaf, never lets down. He swirls through life like a restless comet,
and he does have ideas—worlds of ideas, some of them undoubtedly good ideas. But where has all this incessant activity got him?
Today he is nowhere. Tomorrow he will be in the same place. If
activity alone were all that initiative required, that man today
would be President or at least the head of General Motors Corporation, When I saw him an hour or so ago, still as active, still as
eager, still as surcharged with ideas and enthusiasm as ever, he

said to me: "This time I am going to hit it. I'm on the threshold of my big opportunity. By the way, can you lend me a dollar until Monday?"

So keep in mind the phrase "the right thing." It contains the secret of initiative—of making your ideas work *profitably* for you. Let me give you some examples of men who did the right thing— and reaped the profits I am promising you if you do the right thing.

The prime example of a man of ideas, imagination, initiative is Napoleon. As a young artillery officer, watching what was taking place during the French Revolution, he used his imagination. He saw himself in a position of power. He "did the right thing without being told." Each new opportunity that presented itself gave him another chance to practice initiative—do the right thing. Soon he had conquered Europe. Soon he had made himself Emperor.

He tackled every administrative problem that was brought to him with imagination and forthrightness—and solved it.

The Chancellor of the Exchequer came in one day, worried. He said that France was in bad straits.

"What is the trouble now?" snapped the Emperor.

"It's the finances."

"The finances!" responded Napoleon. "I will take care of the finances!"

And then this man, who was not trained in finance but was a professional soldier, turned his vivid imagination to this new and complex problem with so much effectiveness that he gave France such a sound money system that parts of it are still in use by nations all over the world.

Another respecter of imagination plus initiative was Captain Robert Dollar, the fabulous lumber and shipping magnate of San Francisco. Captain Dollar, by the sheer force of his imagination and persistent initiative, built up a vast empire which still stands. It was he who first saw the possibilities of trade with the Orient— he was applying his imagination. It was he who first capitalized on that trade by sending his ships on regular voyages to the Orient— that was his initiative putting his imagination to work.

Peter B. Kyne has immortalized Captain Robert Dollar in his portrayal of Cappy Ricks, and if you haven't read his saga of initiative entitled *The Go-Getter*, you should.

Let me tell it briefly. Whenever Cappy made ready to select a new man for a responsible position, he gave him a test. It was a test of imagination and initiative, and Cappy called it "the test of the blue vase," because it involved a fifty-cent blue vase. Of the hundreds of men who had taken the test, only one had passed with flying colors. You can see from that that the test was plenty tough.

Then along came Bill Peck, big, one-armed, homely Bill Peck, ex-artilleryman of World War I. Bill went to work for the Ricks interests as salesman, and was so successful that Cappy judged that the time was ripe to give him the blue-vase test.

"Bill, my boy, will you do me a favor?" he asked the salesman, by telephone one Sunday morning.

"Of course, Mr. Ricks. What is it?"

"Bill, there's a blue vase in a shop on Sutter Street that I simply have to have. It's Sunday and I can't get downtown. Will you get it for me, Bill?"

"I certainly will, Mr. Ricks," said Bill Peck.

When he went down to Sutter Street and looked in the shop-window, there was no blue vase. He tried to telephone Cappy. No response. When he went back to take another look, the blue vase was there. But the shop was locked. Bill Peck tried to call the owner, and couldn't reach him. And from then on it was one obstacle right atop another, hours on end. Finally, because he had imagination and initiative, but only after many misadventures, was the ex-artilleryman able to secure the vase. His reward was a job as general manager of an important Ricks property.

The life of every successful man or woman is filled with examples of "doing the right thing without being told" that are almost as dramatic. If you are thinking at this point that the quality of initiative is inborn, I believe I ought to tell you that it is not. It is acquired. It is acquired in the same way that the quality of imagination is acquired—by practice and study. For the rest of this chapter, let me give you some practical and specific suggestions for acquiring it in your life. Ready?

First, try to evaluate your ideas correctly.

Remember now my insistence on the phrase about doing "the right thing" as so essential to initiative? Doing the right thing depends upon deciding what the right thing is. Usually there are several courses open. Which is the right one?

The answer to that question rests upon your ability to evaluate a situation from the facts you have on hand—and to determine what is the most important thing to do next.

How can you learn to determine that, to distinguish the important from the unimportant? One way is to practice seeing things a month, a year, five years hence; project yourself into the future that far in order to determine the relative importance of the ideas you are considering. Another way is to call upon your experience with similar ideas in the past, and judge your present course of action from what happened in the past.

Second, learn to make decisions.

A good many ideas die a-borning because the person who had those ideas is afraid to make a decision concerning them. Most persons, as a matter of fact, are weak on decisions. They take weeks in making up their minds on matters that are not important in the least. But a man or woman with initiative decides.

He or she doesn't always decide correctly, because even the best of people make mistakes. But those with initiative do decide. That is the point I want to make—they decide.

In one office with which I am familiar there is an old blackboard hanging on the wall. Above almost anything else in that firm is this blackboard revered, although its actual value isn't above fifty cents. As a symbol, however, it is worth several million dollars.

It was on that blackboard that the late Henry L. Doherty, utility magnate, then a young executive in a gas company, outlined his plan for a utility empire.

One of Doherty's early associates is a friend of mine, and he likes to tell me what took place in the office that morning. Henry Doherty was always a man with vivid imagination. He thought ten, twenty, thirty years ahead of his associates, and on this particular morning he was having his most grandiose dream.

"We are going to organize a nation-wide utility system with this property as a nucleus," he told his associates. "And this is how we are going to do it."

Whereupon he got up, went over to the blackboard, drew on it an organization chart. Note that, he didn't wait, "think it over a while," wonder, waver, doubt, delay, stew, fret. He decided. He acted upon his decision. Before the day was over, the machinery for that utility empire was in motion. That is imagination plus initiative for you!

There are many times when you cannot make such decisions. I know that. But I also know that there are many other times when you can.

In learning how to decide I have a suggestion for you to follow: decide little things as you go along and don't put anything off if you can possibly avoid it. Once this habit of deciding things becomes a part of your life, you can decide bigger things as easily as you decide the little ones.

Third, start some idea in motion every day.

This is perhaps the hardest of my suggestions, but to get you into the habit of initiated thinking I should like you to start something every day.

Naturally, you won't be able every day to start a world-shaking movement like the American Red Cross or a gigantic business like the Standard Oil Company (two enterprises, by the way, which were only ideas once upon a time but which became realities when initiative was applied to them). If you start just an improved, procedure of doing your work, it will be an achievement in initiative.

You see, all I am attempting in giving you these simple rules is to get you into the habit of initiating your ideas, of doing something to prevent the greatest disaster that can befall any idea, the disaster of having to die a-borning—because someone did not realize that it takes more than imagination to win. It takes imagination plus initiative!

Whenever I think on this subject I like to recollect the story President Lincoln told about General Grant.

"Wherever Grant is," he wrote to a friend, "things always 'git.'"

If you will become the kind of person who has that same kind of ability to make things "git" wherever you are, and then if you will develop your imagination so that there will be more things in your life to make "git," there isn't any reasonable ambition you can have for yourself that you can't attain. You'll have the equipment you need—*imagination plus initiative.*

9

THE MAGIC OF IMAGINATION IN SELLING

The sales manager said, "The best salesman I have on my force is a man who is absolutely devoid of imagination. He's the dumbest cluck I ever saw. Yet he can certainly make sales. If, as you believe, imagination is the first ingredient for successful salesmanship, this man wouldn't be able to sell at all."

Because I (Roth) wanted to see this phenomenon, a salesman without imagination, I asked the sales manager if he could arrange a meeting for me and his top-notch man.

"That'll be easy," he retorted. "How about having lunch with him tomorrow noon?"

"Fine."

So the next noon I spent an hour talking to "the salesman without imagination." Right his sales manager was in saying that this man wasn't brilliant. Large in size, he had a ponderous mind to match his body, and I think that with great justification you could describe him as a man with a low mental ceiling.

But imagination he certainly did have. I reported later to his boss that the salesman not only had imagination, but that he had imagination of the best and most practical kind—he had an objective imagination which showed him clearly what he must say and do on all occasions in order to make sales.

During the course of our luncheon conversation, I asked the salesman if he had any idea why he was so successful. He said yes, he knew exactly why. And his answer proved what I have just told you; namely, that he was a man with a purely objective and practical imagination.

Here is what he told me:

"When I started out on this job, I didn't have any experience or knowledge of selling or of this business. I'm not sure yet whether I was cut out to be a salesman, because I'm not as quick on the trigger as a top-notch salesman is supposed to be. So, I don't know.

"On my first day I asked myself what I would do if I were a buyer and a salesman called on me. What would I like him to be?

"I didn't know it then, but now I see that I was doing the most sensible thing I could possibly do: I was putting myself in the other fellow's shoes, and trying to see myself as the buyer must have seen me.

"I guess the idea must have been sound. It has worked for me for several years, and it still works, so I don't see any reason for changing it.

"Even today, whenever I set out to make calls, I ask myself what I would want to know if I were the buyer. Then I tell the buyer just what I think he would like to hear me say about my goods."

You see, the kind of imagination a salesman has to have in order to succeed this salesman stumbled onto accidentally—the kind of imagination that permits a man to project himself into the prospect's life and see things as his prospect sees them.

Most good salesmen I have known have been highly imaginative men. There is some complaint by sales managers that salesmen are as temperamental as prima donnas. It's true. The fact that good salesmen are temperamental shows that they are surcharged with the imagination necessary to make sales.

On the other hand, some good salesmen are, like the man I have just described to you, rather stolid and easygoing. Nevertheless, these men also have a selling imagination. They have to have one. Every salesman does. It is the prime requisite in a salesman, for a salesman, as I have just told you, has to put himself in the prospect's place in order to sell at all.

Let's go over briefly the steps that take place in every sale, and see how each is taken only with the assistance of imagination.

All good selling starts, as you know, with finding prospects. Finding prospects demands that the salesman apply imagination:

if he cannot imagine who might be a prospect for his goods, he never will have prospects to call upon.

The first thing a good salesman does in analyzing his market to find his prospects is to give his imagination free play. Consciously or unconsciously he asks himself what a prospect has to have or be in order to buy the salesman's goods. Good salesmen take this step automatically. Beginners labor it until they develop that automatic functioning.

One of the most successful salesmen I know sells printing. His chief stock in trade is his ability to get to a printing prospect before any other salesman does. His ability to sense where there's a printing job is uncanny. His competitors are mystified by it. They say he has a sixth sense.

"But I haven't anything any other salesman does not have," this man told me recently. "The only thing under the sun I do that these other boys don't do is study my prospects, analyze their needs, and try to foretell when they're going to be in the market for printing.

"It isn't hard really. All a man has to do is apply a little bit of imagination to the job.

"Sometimes my prospects themselves," he went on, "accuse me of being clairvoyant. I don't disillusion them: if they think I'm a superman it's all right with me. But I can be honest with you. All I do is think a little bit more about my prospects and their possible printing needs. What I do, understand, is put a little bit more of my imagination to work on this job of finding prospects."

And every time you find a salesman who breaks records you'll find a salesman applying this same force of imagination to the job of ferreting out prospects. And every time you find an organization that makes an outstanding success you will also find the same imaginative process hard at work.

I can give you a good example of that in the case of an electric refrigerator manufacturer. Some years ago, before the war, the market for refrigerators was saturated. The industry was worried about its future. The manufacturer I'm telling you about did some imaginative thinking. He asked himself who his best prospects might he. He found the answer: his firm that year doubled its sales.

Other manufacturers in the refrigerator field lost ground. How did he bring about this apparent miracle?

The sales manager was the boy responsible. He figured that if the market for refrigerators among the "natural" or logical prospects (*i.e.*, better-than-average-income families) was saturated, wasn't it foolish to butt your head against a stone wall and try to force your way into that market? What market wasn't saturated? That was his next question. He was using his imagination now, you can see.

He found the answer in the lower income group—a market that had been totally neglected up to that point by manufacturers of electric refrigerators. By addressing itself to that market, with a special refrigerator priced to appeal to lower incomes, the firm rode to its best sales year. That's the magic of imagination again.

After a salesman finds prospects, his next step is to see them. Here again it's an imaginative process. The step of seeing prospects is known in selling parlance as the "approach." This is the simplest of all selling steps, the simplest yet the most important. In less than five minutes I can teach any salesman, provided he will use his imagination, all he needs to know about how to make an approach so effectively that he need never be content with less than 100 per cent attention.

A salesman who uses his imagination at all sees that whenever he calls upon a prospect, he calls as an interloper—he is taking time out of the prospect's life he may have no right to take. The prospect also knows this. Busy as he is, he resents the salesman's interruption, so he uses one of his stock methods for getting rid of the fellow. He says, "Not interested" or "Too busy to talk to you today" or "What do you want? Tell me in fifteen words or less"—or he doesn't even bother to see the salesman: he sends word out he is not in the market.

Every salesman is up against that situation practically every time he makes a call. Unimaginative salesmen are thrown for a loss by it whenever it occurs. Not the salesmen with imagination. With their imagination they know exactly how to prevent it, circumvent it, or whip it.

By what principle do they do this? Remember I told you that a salesman has to use his imagination to put himself in the prospect's place? This is how he does that in his approach. Instead of saying something like this: "I want to show you my goods," he turns it around imaginatively by saying, "Here is your chance to make some money you never dreamed you would be able to make so easily."

Do you see the difference? The first statement aroused no imagination in the prospect's mind whatsoever. But the second set a whole train of imaginative thoughts to work. Money? Of course he wants to make money. Easy money at that. Maybe this salesman has something I had better not miss, concludes the prospect. He lets the salesman in.

There are, of course, technical phases of the approach, such as invoking direct sense appeals, putting something into the hands of the prospect, smiling properly, arousing curiosity; but I judge it will not be necessary to go into those here. All I want to do at this point is show you that in every step of the sale imagination is the king quality.

Another phase of the salesman's life that requires the use of imagination concerns price. Many a good salesman comes a cropper in handling the price phase of his day's work.

"The biggest problem I have with my salesmen," a sales manager remarked to me only last week, "is in getting them to realize the power of price in making sales.

"Almost without exception men develop what is called 'price fear.' They're afraid to quote their prices, and go around hoping maybe the prospect won't ask the price. I try to get my men to use price as a selling weapon, which I believe it to be. But I have a hard time getting them to see my point."

I knew exactly how he felt, because I have had the same problem with most of the salesmen I have known and worked with. A good salesman, however, isn't afraid of price. He sees that if he can invest his selling talk with imagination, no matter what the price is, it will be right.

There are different ways for doing this. One of the most effective—and it is an imaginative technique—is known as "high-price expectation." Before he quotes any price, the salesman builds up his value story. He builds it high. And then he takes another step.

Something like this he says to his prospect: "I have told you about the advantages of these goods. I think that you agree with me, Mr. Freed, that we offer something you need, something no one else can offer you.

"Let me ask you a question: How much would you think a unit that could accomplish as much in your bindery as this can be worth? Would you think that seven hundred dollars is too much to pay for it? Maybe you have in mind a figure like eight hundred dollars or nine hundred dollars. Even at that it will be a bargain."

He waits for the price level he has implanted in the prospect's mind to get itself established there before he goes on. Then he continues, always with a smile:

"But if you act immediately you won't have to pay any such price for this piece of equipment. The price actually is only four hundred and eighty-five dollars."

You can see how imagination has helped this salesman in getting his price into the buyer's consciousness, can't you? By purposely setting a price far higher than he expects to ask, the salesman made his asking price seem low.

Often the use of imagination in quoting the price will be all that is necessary to make the difference between a successful selling operation and one that isn't successful. I have a good example of that for you.

Several years ago a manufacturer of aluminum cooking ware selling direct to the housewives ran into difficulties. Price was his stumbling block. His product, according to the standards of his market, was over-priced—something like fifty dollars for a set of aluminum ware, and a small set at that. The market wasn't conditioned to any such price levels, and the prospects who listened to his salesmen were thinking in terms of twelve dollars or fourteen dollars for a set of kitchen ware, not fifty dollars.

It's customary in handling a situation like this to quote the price only after you have built up the value story, and the manufacturer's salesmen were doing it in the customary way. They were showing the utensils, extolling their merits, building their value high in the minds of the prospect. Then they were springing the price. And that is where the sale bogged down. The price, no matter how much the prospect wanted the kitchen set, was just too high for her to swallow. Failure and frustration were attending the selling efforts of that manufacturer.

Then a sales counselor with an imaginative turn of mind entered the picture. He reversed the pricing process. In place of waiting till they had built up the value story, he had the salesmen hit the prospect with the price first. Quite frankly they told her, "This is an expensive set of kitchen ware. Probably you never in your life ever thought you would see a set of cooking utensils that would be worth fifty dollars. That is the price of this set—fifty dollars."

The prospects were visibly chilled when they heard that, but nevertheless they were curious to see what a fifty-dollar set of aluminum ware was like. So they let the salesman give his talk, his demonstration. The more he talked the less in proportion became the value of the fifty dollars in the lives of the prospects. At the end of twenty or thirty minutes price really became secondary. The salesman had built such a tremendous value story as he went along, you see. That one change of procedure made the organization extremely successful in its operations.

In making a prospect want his goods, which is in reality the genius of salesmanship, a salesman simply arouses the imagination of the prospect until the prospect can see himself enjoying them in his life. This is known as "selling the effect," rather than the goods themselves, as such.

Take the case of an automobile. No good automobile salesman ever talked about his car as so many hundred pounds of steel and aluminum and rubber. The best salesmen dwell very little even upon mechanical excellences. What do they sell? Imaginatively they sell such things as the reputation which comes to a man who owns a car like a Cadillac, the fun he will have next summer driving to the mountains or the beaches, the convenience of driving to town instead of spending long hours on busses. That is what we mean by selling the effect.

To the extent that the salesman can make the prospect see himself behind the wheel of that car, enjoying the prestige that ownership gives him, having all the conveniences, he makes sales. And selling the effect is entirely a matter of arousing the prospect's imagination, don't you see?

Consider the final stage of every sale—the close. The salesman is ready now to take the order. If he is a good salesman he lets imagination play a dominant role. He uses a time-tested closing technique, selecting one from several he has on tap. All these closing techniques are built around imagination.

The simplest closing technique is that of assumption. The salesman assumes that his prospect will buy. In place of using the word "if" in referring to the prospect and his possession and use of the goods, the salesman always politely uses the word "when"—in itself imaginative, because it gives the prospect a chance to picture himself owning the goods.

One of the effective uses of assumption consists in getting the prospect to agree upon some minor detail, and when he agrees upon the detail he has agreed to buy the goods.

This is the way it works out. The salesman says: "Will you have these shipped by express or freight?" in place of saying, "Will you buy my goods or won't you?" You can see how imaginative the first question is, how unimaginative the second. He asked the prospect how he wants the goods shipped. The prospect sees the goods on the way to his factory or his home. He decides to get them in a hurry, so he has them shipped by express. And when he decides that, he agrees to buy.

Another closing that depends entirely upon imagination makes use of some impending event. It's a darling of the skilled salesmen, this close is. When they judge the time is ripe for trying to close, they say something like this: "There's a price change coming on the fifteenth; don't know how much the boost is going to be, but I judge it'll be plenty stiff. Tell you what, you give me your order now and I'll get it under the wire, so you won't have to pay a premium."

But I think of all the closing techniques good salesmen use the one which comes closest to depending upon pure imagination is known as the "narrative technique." In using it the salesman, at the moment of closing, merely tells his prospect a story—the story of a prospect whose conditions paralleled his own, a prospect who found profit, satisfaction, in buying the salesman's goods.

"I suppose you know the firm of Thomas and Cohan over at Big Rapids, don't you?" the salesman asks. "Oh, yes," responds the prospect.

Then the salesman is off on his story: the first time he talked to these alert partners, they weren't too enthusiastic over his line. They didn't think it would sell. It was maybe a little too high-priced for the market. So they hesitated about taking it on.

"But I was talking to Mr. Thomas last Tuesday," the salesman goes on, "and what a story he told me!"

And then the prospect hears the story—a story of quick turn-over, large profits, satisfied customers, increased prestige, all the result of having bought the salesman's products.

As he sits there and listens to that story, the prospect sees himself enjoying the quick turnover, the large profits, the satisfied customers, the increased prestige. So he just has to buy. His imagination makes the sale for the salesman, once the salesman sets that imagination in motion.

Good salesmen use imagination in another way in their selling too: they ask questions. At least one run-down store was restored to greatness because the talented woman who took over the store saw the value of asking its customers questions. This woman, Hortense N. Odlum, took over a New York department store in bad condition. The first thing she did was to train her salespeople to ask customers what they wanted to buy and how they wanted it sold to them. In a short time she trebled the business.

An automobile manufacturer found that he could train his salesmen to use their imagination by suggesting such simple questions as these: "Don't you like the feel of this car on the road?" "What do you like most about the interior of this car?"

These simple questions put the prospect definitely into the picture by their appeal to his imagination and to his ego and by making him feel he was a participant in the selling function. Sales mounted.

Another important phase of the salesman's life has to do with handling the objections which the prospect brings up. Here again it's a job for imagination. Instead of buying, the prospect interposes an objection: "Your price is too high" or "I can buy the same thing for less elsewhere" or "I don't like the color" or "My friend bought one and it didn't stand up" or "I don't believe the cleaner will do everything you say it will." Statements like these are called "objections." Unless a salesman knows how to handle them, handle them imaginatively, he isn't going to make sales.

But good salesmen do not fear objections. They like them. They welcome them. For every objection gives a salesman the opportunity to put a little bit more imagination into his selling process.

There are a number of ways to handle objections. Here is the way an imaginative salesman does it: When the prospect brings up his objection, the salesman doesn't answer him right off. He pauses. The pause has an important part in every step of the sale. It unpoises the buyer. It sets the buyer's imagination to working, because he doesn't know exactly what the salesman is going to say when he does talk. Now the salesman smiles. That also is important, a smile: shows the buyer that the salesman is still friendly, wants to be friendly.

With the stage properly set by the pause and the smile, the salesman is ready to get ahead and handle the objection. The best salesmen use a question for this purpose.

They ask, "Why do you say you don't believe this machine will do all I have said it will?" That puts the prospect on the defensive. And then the salesman, using facts and good humor, answers the prospect's objections, and usually sells in spite of them.

Because imagination is so important in good selling, salesmen who make records spend most of their lives studying prospects, how prospects are going to react to their words. They, in other words, try all the time to put themselves in the other fellow's place.

As head of a large organization, a man I know is busy, but he still insists on spending a good many hours studying people. Often he will spend an evening talking to a truck driver whose acquaintance he has scraped up, or, dressed in old clothes, prowling through the lower part of town, rubbing elbows with all sorts of people.

Some of his associates think that the "old man" is a little bit touched to "throw himself away" on these so-called lower classes. But the old man himself doesn't look upon it in that light. Behind his practice there is some sound, fundamental business thinking.

"Unless you stay tuned in on people," he remarked to me the other day, "and that doesn't mean on the men who belong to the same clubs—it means all people—how can you expect to serve them? It's only when you study people that you can understand their wants."

I happen to know that most of the shrewd advertising and merchandising ideas which have catapulted his firm to such greatness during the past decade originate with the president himself. And he told me frankly that these ideas come to him from keeping in tune with people.

About this there is nothing new, of course. All wise leaders—political and religious as well as business—know that they have to "keep the common touch."

The late Daniel Frohman called his practice of keeping tuned in "listening in the lobby." Between acts each night he would stand quietly in the lobby of his theater, listening to comments on the play. W. D. Estey, brilliant young advertising executive, kept tuned in by spending his summers as a barker for a Coney Island sideshow.

One man who has given a great deal of time and thought to the value of imagination in business says that the very words you use, depending upon the amount of imagination they invoke, determine your success in making sales. Elmer Wheeler is this man's name. His specialty is studying words.

Some of the things Wheeler has done with his use of words are almost fantastic. He sold millions of square clothespins, for instance, with the use of three words: "They won't roll." Indian moccasins for boys didn't take hold until Wheeler's magic words went to work. "The kind the real Indians wear, sonny," the salesman said—and sales increased. White shoe polish sales went up when the salesman said, "It won't rub off." Telling a woman that a large-size package of soap powder was the "family economical size" increased sales 300 per cent.

Wheeler sums up his twenty-year search for words that would make sales in a short, sententious sentence: "Consider the prospect's response to what you say."

What that means is simply that you should project your imagination beyond the mere words you use on your prospect, and think of his response to your words. And that is the cardinal rule of all good selling. Put yourself in your prospect's place, think as your prospect thinks—and then say and do the things that will cause him to think favorably about you and your goods. That is the genius of salesmanship.

10
Imagination in Advertising

One of the best salesmen I (Woolf) have ever known is a man who sells insurance. Not long ago I asked him how he did it.

"I am sure you have heard the story," he replied, "about the farmer who lost one of his animals—a donkey, I believe it was. A neighbor gave him this advice: 'Just try to imagine, Hiram, that you are that donkey. Having run away, where would you most likely be right now?'

"Hiram fell into a state of self-hypnosis, succeeded in imagining himself to be the missing donkey, thought of a nice lush pasture where he would like to be, went there, found the beast and led him home.

"In selling," continued my friend, "I always try to imagine I am the fellow I am talking to. I try to listen with his ears to what I am saying. I endeavor to think of his problems as being my problems and what I would do about them if I were in his shoes. I try to think of his family as my family, his salary as my salary, his needs and desires and fears and frustrations as my own."

My friend, reflecting, was silent for a moment. "I think," he said, "it is purely a matter of imagination, the ability to think with the other fellow's mind and heart."

What this successful insurance man said sums up my whole philosophy of advertising. I was reminded, as he spoke, of a story about two bootblacks related by Lorin F. Deland in his excellent little book on imagination in business. (*Imagination in Business*: Harper's.)

One Saturday afternoon he found these two boys, who were about the same age, standing on opposite sides of a crowded street in Springfield. So far as he could judge, there was no preference for either side of the street, for an equally large crowd seemed to be moving on both sides. The bootblacks had no regular stand, but each had his box slung over his shoulder, and, standing on the curb-stone, solicited passers-by to stop and have a shine. Each boy had one "call," a method of solicitation repeated at regular intervals. The two solicitations were entirely different, but each was composed of four words. Neither of the boys ever varied his. Yet one of these boys by the peculiar wording of his call, seemed to be getting twice as much business as the other, and Deland watched them for a long time.

The cry of the first boy was "Shine your boots here." The cry of the second boy was "Get your Sunday shine!" It was then Saturday afternoon, and the hour was four o'clock. The second boy, declared Deland, employed imagination.

Consciously or unconsciously, this second lad had succeeded in imagining himself to be the "donkey." Here were crowds of people hurrying by with bundles under their arms. Where were they going? Home, of course! What was in those bundles? Why, new clothes, at least in a lot of them. The next day would be Sunday and these folks would dress up in their Sunday finery, go to church, visit with their friends, call on their best girls, have the preacher for dinner.

Naturally enough, our second boy reasoned, some of these people will want a Sunday shine if I only suggest it to them. That's what I would want if I were in their shoes.

Well, that's about all there is to imagination in advertising—the ability to put yourself in the other fellow's shoes.

When you sit down with a pencil to write words designed to sell an item of merchandise, or perhaps a service, start, always, by imagining yourself to be the donkey.

We hear a lot about *ideas* in advertising. We must be careful not to let that word fool us.

An idea does not necessarily have merit just because it is an idea. It may be clever, cute, catchy, easy to remember, and yet not be worth a Confederate dollar in the sale and advertising of your product.

Beware of the advertising idea which has no discernible merit but its cleverness. Not that "catchy" ideas have nothing to recommend them. They do. But they have merit only when they relate your product to a human need.

"The Prudential has the strength of Gibraltar" is probably one of the best known and most effective slogans in the world. It is adroit, arresting, memorable. But its "cleverness" is only a small part of its worth.

Security is a great human hunger. A hundred fears beset man, and one of the greatest of them is the dread of financial insecurity. Millions of people have lost their savings as the result of bank failures, building and loan association crashes, or busted real estate booms.

The Prudential slogan is an idea. But what makes it good is that it is right on the target of a passionate human longing.

Once a business associate of mine, the late S. Ronald Hall, a very able advertising man, had occasion to sell his Scranton home. Times were none too good, nobody knew what was ahead, and money was so tight there was practically no home-buying activity. Hall placed the sale of the house with a large and reputable real-estate firm, but after a month of effort results were nil. Buyers were cautious, holding on to their money.

So Hall took matters in his own hands, wrote a display ad, six or seven inches over two columns, and ran it in the Scranton *Times*.

To most people, buying a house is like buying a pig in a poke. The average layman, forced to rely pretty much on the honesty of the seller, can be fooled easily enough.

"Now I wonder," asked Hall of himself, "what would appeal to me if I were a prospective buyer instead of a seller." Putting himself in the other fellow's shoes, Hall reasoned that what would appeal to him most of all was assurance that he would be getting honest value for his money.

The copy Hall put together for that ad was frankness in the extreme. "I hope you will like this house," he wrote, "and I really think you will. But maybe not. There are likely some things you won't care for. My wife thinks the kitchen is too small, there is a spare attic bedroom we have never been able to heat satisfactorily, and after a hard rain the cellar is damp for a week." Then he went on to praise enthusiastically the good things about the house. "So you see," his copy concluded, "it's a beautiful house and it's sturdily built, and I honestly believe my price makes it a fine investment. But I do want you to know of its faults, just to make sure you won't be dissatisfied afterwards."

As I recall it, Hall's ad produced more than two hundred prospective buyers, and the sale was quickly made. The previous conventional ads, written by the real-estate agents, produced not a flicker of interest.

Here you see a fine example of imaginative thinking in advertising. Hall's advertisement struck a responsive chord because he thought in terms of the other fellow's interests and point of view.

Consider the case of Lifebuoy soap. Its odor suggested a strong disinfectant and the public was turning against it in favor of bland white soaps such as Ivory and Lux. Scented soaps such as Cashmere Bouquet, and "beauty treatment" soaps such as Woodbury's, were also giving Lifebuoy increasingly severe competition.

Conventional advertising appeals failed to halt the sales decline. It seemed that people just didn't want the product. Unless it could somehow be related to a human hankering, unless people could be persuaded that Lifebuoy gave them something they wanted, it seemed unlikely that advertising could be made to pay.

Here was a job for imagination. Mere "inventions"—trick slogans, jingles, cartoons, and all the clever little artifices and stratagems that pass for imagination in so much current advertising—would certainly fail. Such devices as double-your-money-back offers, premiums, two-cakes-for-the-price-of-one appeals, attractive extra-profit deals to merchants, and so on, might result in some temporary sales stimulation, but no more than that. Such devices never have made—and never will make—a permanent success of a product the public doesn't want.

The answer was found in the famous "B.O." campaign. This idea, which plays on the theme of how each of the two sexes can be more attractive to the other, came out of keen imaginative insight into human motivation and behavior. The clever "B.O." tagging of the theme, plus the physical dress of the ads (cartoons and blurbs), were most useful inventions, but it was the power of the basic idea—*how to get your man*—that put real pull into the campaign.

Advertising is at its best when it stirs the imagination of the reader or listener. In another book of mine I wrote that "It is probably not going too far to say that no sale is ever made until the buyer has first imagined himself as the owner. . . . Automobile salesmen know the value of this principle. Realizing how difficult it is to interest the prospect when they talk to him in his office or his home, they concentrate their efforts on the business of persuading him to take a demonstration ride. Once the prospect is behind the wheel, the salesman knows his chance of making a sale is immeasurably increased. The prospect is no longer an inactive and impersonal observer on the sidelines; he is an actor and not a spectator of the game. He is now in a position to imagine himself as the owner of the car, and he finds himself, often unwittingly, thinking about how he will use it and enjoy it. The car has now become a concrete part of his experience; he is no longer able to think of it impersonally."

Words and pictures that succeed in visualizing for the reader the product in use in this manner go a long way toward making the sale. Try, as you write an ad, to give the reader a moment of experience as the happy owner of the product. If you have ever leaned back in your chair and, abandoning yourself to revery, have imagined yourself as the possessor of a fine country estate or as the owner of a Rolls-Royce or as the president of a bank, or as having something you have always wanted, you will realize the importance of arousing the reader in the same way with the words and pictures you use in advertising.

Words themselves can be imagination stimulators—picture-painters. Consider, as you write, the *connotation* as well as the denotation of words.

Arlo Bates says, "In the familiar line of Wordsworth,
　　　　　　　'A violet by a mossy stone,'
the words denote a certain common flower beside a stone covered with another common and ordinary vegetable growth; they connote all the beauty of the azure blossom, the sweetness of the spring

tide, the quietude of a sylvan scene, all those lovely and touching associations which can be expressed only by suggestion."

What you seek to do is to create images in the mind of your listener or reader. Some words are almost totally lacking in power of imagery, whereas other words—*specific* words—are potent picture-painters.

By employing a specific term, says Herbert Spencer, an appropriate image can at once be suggested and a more vivid impression provided. To write that "John *walked* down the street" is to create a faint picture. But to say that "John

— waddled	— or teetered
— or toddled	— or staggered
— or minced	— or reeled
— or strutted	— or sauntered
— or strolled	— or idled
— or ambled	— or hopped

down the street" is to suggest with one specific word an appropriate image of John's manner of gait.

It is wrong to assume that your copy is objective, that it is written from the point of view of your reader, just because it has the "you" approach. You can "you" the reader until he cries for mercy and still fail to get under his skin.

If you are a grocer and have a big stock of watermelons to sell, here is an ad you might try:

> I Know How a Boy Looks
> With a Yard-Long Slice of
> Watermelon
> I know how a prize watermelon looks when it is sunning its fat rotundity among pumpkin vines and 'simblins'; I know how to tell when it is ripe without 'plugging' it; I know how inviting it looks when it is cooling itself in a tub of water under the bed, waiting; I know how it looks when it lies on the table in the sheltered great floor space between house and kitchen, and the children gathered for the sacrifice

and their mouths watering; I know the cracking sound it makes when the carving knife enters its end, and I can see the split flying along in front of the blade as the knife cleaves its way to the other end; I can see its halves fall apart and display the rich red meat and the black seeds, and the heart standing up, a luxury fit for the elect; I know how a boy looks behind a yard-long slice of the melon, and I know how he feels; for I have been there. I know the taste of the watermelon that has been honestly come by, and I know the taste of the watermelon which has been acquired by art. Both taste good, but the experienced know which tastes best.

John Smith, Grocer

There is an ad that rouses the imaginations and excites the taste buds—*your* taste buds—and yet there is not a "you" in it. John Smith didn't write it, though. The name of the adman is Mark Twain.

Make a practice of studying reflectively the advertising you see in magazines and newspapers and hear on the radio. How much imagination—the kind of imagination Hiram used when he found his lost donkey—did the writer use? Analyze the headlines, the appeals. You will find hundreds of examples that fall short. Here is one, in a current magazine on my desk, that has little to recommend it. The product advertised is a fountain pen, the ad covers a half page in a popular magazine, the headline reads: *Dependable Performance.*

Can you think of one valid reason why anybody should read the copy that follows? Who can say that this "idea" promises to fill an unfilled hankering? Who upon reading "Dependable Performance" can say, his eyes lighting up, that he was motivated to turn to his wife and ejaculate, "By golly, Susie, this is it! I've been waiting for a dependable performer since I went to high school!"

"Every man is really two men," once wrote Lord Chesterfield, "the man he is and the man he wants to be." This second man is the man you are writing to. Here's where your imagination can count most heavily.

11
Trade Names, Trade-marks, Slogans

It would be difficult to overestimate the importance of the "symbols"—trade names, trade-marks, firm names, slogans—which identify your company and its products or services in the mind of the consumer.

And this is true whether your business is a roadside hamburger stand or a transcontinental airline, or your product a cake of soap or a kitchen stove.

In Chapter Two it was stated that there is perhaps no greater challenge to the imaginative mind than the selection of trade symbols. It was stated further that the quality of imagination displayed by businessmen in the naming of products and services is appallingly second rate.

It will profit us in this present chapter to examine the problem in some detail. Let us see if we can agree on what it is that makes some symbols so appealing and memorable. Are there any clear principles to guide us in our selection?

I (Woolf) think there are. Effective symbols are the inventions of the creative brain *that has a thorough understanding of what interests people and why.*

Let us make this clear with a simple example. Most human beings have an intense interest in animals. Nearly all families have a pet—a dog, a cat, a canary, a goldfish. A crowd of people, grownups as well as children, will stand for a quarter of an hour watching the antics of an organ-grinder's monkey. Great throngs will crane their necks for an hour or more watching firemen rescue a bewildered kitten from high up in a tree. Periodicals of huge circulation such as the *Reader's Digest* make a practice of including animal stories in practically every issue.

Animals, in short, are one of the things that interest people.

L. C. Probert, Chesapeake and Ohio vice-president, knew of this great human interest when he dreamed up the railroad's beloved cat "Chessie." And in doing this, as pointed out in Chapter Two, he performed a notable act of business imagination.

Twenty-three years ago there was printed in newspapers everywhere news of the death of a man who painted one of the world's most celebrated pictures.

The subject of this picture is a dog—a little white fox terrier with black ears, head cocked, eyes puzzled, as he listens to his master's voice coming from the horn of a talking machine. "His Master's Voice," painted by Francis Barraud, was not originally made for commercial purposes. Barraud, entranced by the behavior of his little dog, Nipper, on hearing a talking machine, did the painting for art's sake.

The picture became a famous trade-mark because somebody in the Gramophone Company, Ltd., of London, knew what interested people. Realizing the tremendous human appeal of the little dog, he bought the painting from Barraud for his company. Later, "His Master's Voice" came to America when the Victor Company acquired a controlling interest in the English company.

Barraud's puzzled fox terrier is the best known dog today in the whole wide world, Napoleon and Lassie not excluded. His owners, who list him as one of their most valuable assets, have instructed firemen that the first thing to save, in case of fire, is Barraud's original painting of Nipper.

The camel as a trade-mark for a cigarette was conceived by R. J. Reynolds, a great lover of animals, who understood their great appeal to people.

Only a very modest advertising fund was available for the launching of Kools in 1923. Small ads—quarter pages in black and white—had to fight the big color pages of competitors for attention, and that took some doing. An attention-attracting, interest-compelling element was sorely needed. Again an animal was the answer—that droll and debonair penguin, Mr. Kool. The public took the captivating little bird to its heart—the advertising caught on in record time. Mr. Kool, incidentally, sets the style in the penguin "body beautiful": he is much plumper and jollier than the real-life bird, and many artists, preferring him to nature's own version, use him as a model.

But animals are only one of many, many things that interest people. In story and song the charms of simple rustic life "down on the farm" are forever being eulogized. Even city dwellers who have never been west of the Hudson dream wistfully of spending the rest of their days in the country. And erstwhile rustics, now big-city folks, pine away with nostalgic yearning for the little red schoolhouse and the joys of the groaning farm table.

Hence it is that we find Log Cabin as a name for molasses and sirup; Jones Little Dairy Farm for sausages; Grandma's Old Fashioned for molasses; Meadow Gold, Brookfield, and Land O'Lakes as names for butter; Deerfoot Farms for sausage and bacon; Catskill Mountain for smoked turkey and sausage; Old Homestead for ham and bacon; and Pride of the Farm for catsup and tomato juice. In Aunt Jemima as a name for pancake flour, in Maxwell House for coffee, and in Rastus as a trade-mark for Cream of Wheat, we see appeals aimed at the prevailing belief that the old South, Negro cooks, and good food are synonymous.

People are interested in gayety, lightheartedness, fun. There are some types of products—little things that are bought for the pleasure of the moment at a cost of only a few pennies—that should not be too heavy and serious in their bid for public favor. A man who wants a Kuppenheimer suit is not likely to ask for a "kup"; but somehow when he wants to drink a Coca-Cola it seems perfectly fitting to say, "Gimme a coke."

Consider, then, the mood people are probably in most frequently when they buy your product. If it is a trifling pleasure-of-the-moment product that sounds like fun, try for symbols that fit the mood. This has been done most effectively, I think, in the candy field, and here are a few popular names in evidence thereof: Chuckles, Baffle Bar, Charms, Baby Ruth, Jolly Jack, Love Nest, Payday, Power House, Life Savers, Snickers, Forever Yours, Dreams, Tootsie Rolls, Hi-mac, Jolly Time (popcorn), and Crackerjack.

The most insistent urge that motivates the human race is, as everybody knows, the good old biological one. There is seemingly no limit to the length human beings will go in response to the proddings of sex hunger. The makers of perfumes have, more than any other type of advertiser, capitalized on this human weakness, if weakness it is, in creating names for their products. On any toilet goods counter there will be found on sale provocative essences with such names as My Sin, Naughtiness, Shameless, After Dark, Tantalizing, Dangerous, Seductive. Few advertisers in other fields, including women's clothing and accessories, have gone as far as perfumers in this direction—which is probably just as well. But the principle they follow in naming their products does show that they know what interests people—and why.

If your product is one that is superior in a special point of advantage to the consumer, and if you desire to give this selling point continuous emphasis, you may find it desirable to emphasize it with your trade name, your trade-mark, or your slogan. The little chick breaking out of its shell, which is the Bon Ami trade-mark, together with the legend "Hasn't scratched yet," illustrates the principle admirably. Another example, already mentioned, gives double emphasis to the major selling idea—first, with the name itself, Kools; second, with the little trade-mark character, Mr. Kool. The name Cream of Wheat for a cereal suggests the smooth, creamy texture of the product, which is one of its distinctive characteristics. Softasilk, as a name for a cake flour, is very suggestive, and so is Rice Krispies as a name for an exceptionally crisp dry-rice cereal. Another fine suggestive name is Tender Leaf brand as a name for a tea.

It is amazing how little imagination has been used in the naming of beverages, both of beers and of soft drinks. Unlike candy and food advertisers, beverage makers have been content to go along on exceedingly conventional lines. Considered strictly on their merit as names, and forgetting that years of advertising have given them their present significance, I think it is fair to say that the following symbols for beer are as dull, as unprovocative, and as uninspiring as barley water: Acme, Regal, Budweiser, Atlas Prager, Blatz, Breidt's, Carling's, Burger, Coors, Drewry's. I can't think of one beer that has an imaginative name. In the soft drink category I find, with the possible exception of White Rock, not a single case of a name that is in any way suggestive or appealing along the lines being discussed in this chapter.

It is true, of course, that many products and services do not easily lend themselves to fanciful, imaginative names. Certainly it would seem little short of reckless to eschew such names as Cadillac and Buick and to christen cars with such names as Flying Rabbit, Blue Streak, or White Flash. Still, a little more imagination might pay dividends. While its war record is probably the major reason for its success, Jeep as a name for the Willys car has surely caught the public's fancy. The airplane manufacturers, with such names as Black Widow and Thunderbolt, have fewer inhibitions.

It has long been my belief that the names of most services and institutions are utterly lacking in suggestiveness and distinction of any kind, for example, the following names of ten different and competing insurance companies:

> National Aid Life Insurance Company
> National Benefit Insurance Association
> The National Board of Fire Underwriters
> National Fire Insurance Group
> National Fire Insurance Company
> The National Life & Accident Insurance Company,
>   Inc.
> National Mutual Benefit Legal Reserve Life Insur-
>   ance Company
> National Protective Insurance Company
> National Surety Corporation
> National Union Fire Insurance Company

I have before me a list of all of the important insurance companies in the United States. Out of the lot I find only two that show an attempt at originality and distinction: the Square Deal Insurance Company and the New World Insurance Company. This same dreadful lack of imagination is seen in names of hotels: Bedford, Buffalo, Californian, Cleveland, Kenmore, Philadelphian. The list is endless. There are some eating places that do better, as mentioned in Chapter Two, with such names as The Farm Cupboard and Johnny Cake Inn.

Retail stores and retail service establishments of every description are probably the least original of all. Main Street in every city in America is crowded with hopeful merchants who make their bid for attention with such firm names as Smith's Hardware Store, Brownsville Mercantile Company, Webster's Haberdashery. I hold to the view that a suggestive and interest-arousing name will do much to attract customers to a store. There is in Santa Fe, New Mexico, an Indian gift shop, a store which I helped to establish, that operates under the name of The Shop of the Rainbow Man. This name is derived from that of the Zuñi god, the Rainbow Man, highly revered for his beneficence to man. I can testify that this distinctive name, featured on billboards, in newspapers, and on the air, has been effective in bringing business to the shop. I am convinced that if a name such as Sante Fe Gift Store or The Palace Avenue Gift Store had been the symbol selected, the shop would not have caught the public fancy as quickly as it did. The fact that local people refer to the store as the "Rainbow Man" or the "Rainbow Shop" is all to the good. I am convinced that people feel more friendly to a name that they can revise and refashion to suit their own tastes. Try to remodel The New Mexican Mercantile Company into something familiar, easy to say and easy to remember, and see where you get!

Rainbow Man has one additional point of merit: it lends itself readily to pictorialization. A stylized picture of the Zuñi god appears on a sign in front of the shop, on billboards and other advertising matter, even on letterheads, labels, and wrapping paper. When you are coining a name for a product or a business firm try your imagination on a symbol that can be interestingly and dramatically pictorialized.

Here are some examples you may find suggestive: Log Cabin sirup (can resembling a miniature log cabin); Camel cigarettes (picture of a camel on the package) Quaker Oats (picture of the old Quaker on the package); Four Roses whisky (picture of four red roses not only on the bottle but in every advertisement and on all point-of-sale display material).

A few paragraphs back I stated that retail stores are probably the worst offenders of all. On second thought I believe that newspapers deserve the green banana. Being merchants in words and supposedly wise in what interests people and why, they of all people might be expected to exercise imagination and ingenuity in naming their ware.

I have on my desk a copy of the newspaper section of *Standard Rate & Data Service*, a thick volume which lists every newspaper of consequence in the United States and its possessions. Following are all of the newspaper names that appear on the first four pages:

Anniston *Star*   Opelika *News*
Birmingham *News*   Selma *Times-Journal*
Birmingham *Age-Herald*   Sheffield *Tri-Cities Daily*
Decatur *Daily*   Talladego *Home*
Dothan *Eagle*   Troy *Messenger*
Florence *Times*   Tuscaloosa *Times*
Gadsden *Times*   Anchorage *Times*
Huntsville *Times*   Cordova *Times*
Mobile *Press*   Fairbanks *News-Miner*
Mobile *Register*   Juneau *Empire*
Montgomery *Advertiser*   Ketchikan *Chronicle*
Montgomery *Journal*

"*Times*" appears seven times in the first four pages of the book, with five hundred pages still to go! If the average held up, a full tabulation would probably reveal approximately nine hundred *Times* papers in the United States, plus heaven only knows how many more in the country weeklies and small dailies.

This pitiful dearth of imagination by newspapermen in naming their products, this lack of understanding of what interests people, is evident everywhere in every branch of American business. So many businessmen, big and little, seem to be utterly indifferent to the magic and the power of words. If they have any appreciation at all of the pleasing and persuasive implications and connotations of words, they fail completely to show it so many,

many times. A man must be "word-deaf" indeed when he creates a lovely piece of glassware and calls it Congress Crystal or Sterling Brand or some other such thing; or when he weaves a beautiful rug and calls it Leadership Loom; or when he invests thousands of dollars on the *décor* of his smart new store and calls it Jackson's Dress Shop. But that is exactly what happens much of the time.

Frequently businessmen, going too far in their eagerness to be original, come up with such mysterious enigmas as Alseco, Kysite, Ka-Bar, Mac-Rac, Rotorex, Escolite, Myst-O, Calart. I find upon investigation that what Calart really means is "California Artificial" and that it is used as a trade name for synthetic flowers. But who would ever guess it? Such words, in my opinion, have little value; they denote nothing, connote nothing, paint no pictures, have no common point of interest with the consumer, are hard to pronounce, difficult to remember. These names, mere inventions, are not the end result of fine imaginative thinking of the kind we are considering here.

Sometimes the coiner of words, straining hard to create a name that will describe the function and superiority of his product, arrives at weird results. I have figured out that Pro-Tex-Sil (a polish) is supposed to mean "protects silver" and that Renuzit (a cleaner) means "renews it," but the effort to decipher these word puzzles puts a strain upon my attention and my patience. Iernoz (a head treatment of some sort, I gather) may mean "eye, ear, and nose," but your guess is as good as mine. Kelp-I-Dine, a concoction for reducing, may mean the ashes of seaweed, but who knows?

Effective symbols—trade names, trade-marks, firm names, slogans—are produced by the creative brain that has *a thorough understanding of what interests people and why*. If you can originate a symbol that will strike a responsive chord in people, you may shorten the road to success. Of course, almost any name—Kodak, Packard, Esso, Kotex—can be made significant in the public mind when large sums of money have been spent, over a period of years, for advertising. However, happy choice of a name and a trade-mark is often a short cut.

12
THE WONDERFUL ART OF SHOWMANSHIP

His secretary phoned me (Woolf) (from New York to Chicago) that Mr. Elwood wanted an hour of my time three weeks hence, at eleven-fifteen o'clock in the morning.

On the appointed day Mr. Elwood made his appearance at precisely fifteen minutes after eleven. He was dressed in formal morning clothes—cutaway coat, black-and-white striped trousers, a white carnation for a boutonniere, a shiny gold-topped stick in his hand.

On his heels was a colored page boy, brilliantly uniformed from the top of his pate to the toes of his shoes, lugging a large and impressive looking portfolio.

Who was Mr. Elwood? He was the ambassador extraordinary of a company organized to promote the sale of unsettled land in the Southwest to small farmers and ranchers. Mr. Elwood's mission was that of selling stock in the enterprise, and he is said to have been enormously successful.

Whatever the secret of the Elwood brand of persuasion, he was emphatically a showman. Phoning a thousand miles three weeks ahead of time instead of using a three-cent stamp . . . his secretary specifying not eleven o'clock, not eleven-thirty, but eleven-*fifteen* . . . the cutaway coat, the boutonniere and cane, the dazzling page. That was showmanship—showmanship that worked.

When Franklin Roosevelt, breaking precedent, flew to Chicago in 1932 to accept the Democratic nomination, his act was one of superb and memorable showmanship.

When Major Goethals took charge of building the Panama Canal, he amazed everybody by casting aside his uniform and appearing in plain and modest mufti. Soldiers and diplomats were shocked, but the large force of civilian native laborers were pleased and re-assured. That was showmanship planned for a purpose—and it did the trick.

When Leonard Wood became governor of Cuba, he walked down Santiago's sun-baked main thoroughfare solemnly swinging a Catholic censer, a Catholic canopy shading his Protestant head, a mitered bishop at his side. Here, again, was astute showman-ship—and the crowds cheered madly.

I like the story about Cyrus McCormick. Out to capture England as a market for his binder, he decided to show it against compet-ing machines at the big London agricultural show.

He was beset by ill luck right off. His machine, taken across on a ship that was partially wrecked, was dumped off at the dock rusty, dirty, battered up. McCormick, knowing that competing machines would be brightly painted and beribboned, had to think sharp.

There still was time to do a refurbishing job, but McCormick's sense of drama, his feeling for people, ruled against it. Dilapidated horses dragged his unlovely contraption into the arena—and the huge crowd gasped with astonishment. Such is the Englishman's love of the underdog in any sporting event that McCormick's binder, winning hands down, was the talk of London for days.

Showmanship does it! But you need not be a great man or a president or a general, or be faced with a great crisis, to use it. If your success hangs on influencing other people, no matter how ordinary your job or your business, you should be on the alert for chances to use a little of the magic of showmanship.

When William Wrigley, a green young salesman, was peddling soap to French-Canadian storekeepers, he introduced himself in each store by tapping his chest dramatically and shouting, "*Savon mineral!*" ("Mineral soap!"). This was all the French young Wrigley knew, but it delighted the merchants to be greeted in their own tongue. Seemingly a small thing, this bit of "theater," but Mr. Wrig-ley is on record that it performed wonders.

Celebrated among travelers is a little eating place in Las Vegas, Nevada, known as "Doc's." It is tiny, twenty-five feet by twenty-four; its furniture is plain; its floor bare; and it is situated on the "wrong side of the tracks." Yet tourists, many of them celebrities in their own right, have been known to drive a hundred miles out of their way to sit at Doc's linoleum-covered counter.

The food is superb, of course. But what has contributed equally to Edward Ladd's fame is his shrewd showmanship. A hearty, lusty ex-Texan, he booms, "Hi yuh, neighbor," to each incoming diner. He calls his place a "joint," his lunch "noon chuck," and his menu "pizen chart." His hamburger steak is an "honest half pound of chopped round" for "one buck."

On one wall is painted: "Heaven sends us good meat—The devil sends us cooks." On the wall opposite Doc invites his guests to "Squat a piece, Neighbor, and rest your saddle."

He "editorializes" picturesquely in a column on his menus and they are collector's items, prized by connoisseurs the world over.

But don't get the idea that Doc Ladd is an untamed cowboy turned restaurateur. He learned to fix food at the Canton in London and was awarded his master's degree as *chef de cuisine* in Paris. He is as sophisticated as they come. His showmanship is carefully thought out and his every act is calculated to add to the "personality" of his "joint."

Charles H. Walgreen, founder of the great chain of retail drugstores, knew the value of the dramatic in his dealings with people. He started his business with a small neighborhood store in Chicago. One of his first orders came over the telephone from a housewife who lived within a few doors of his store.

Mr. Walgreen relayed her order in a whisper to an assistant, telling him to rush delivery to her. Meantime, he prolonged his telephone conversation with his new customer.

Within three or four minutes she interrupted the conversation, explaining that the doorbell was ringing. Quickly she returned to the phone and told Mr. Walgreen excitedly that her order had already arrived.

"That's just an example, madam," Mr. Walgreen told her, "of Walgreen service."

A young Chicago friend of mine not long ago won the job he wanted because he applied a touch of showmanship. Seeking a berth on the editorial staff of a New York trade journal, a letter from the managing editor told him there was no hurry and "to drop in any time during the next month or two if you happen to be in New York." My friend hastened that very day to the airport, sent a wire that he was on his way via plane, and was waiting before the editor's door the next morning.

Although there was no immediate opening, the wire and the plane was too much for the editor and he succumbed to such astonishing hustle and initiative. Showmanship paid off.

I know a clerk in a cigar store who, when he takes a box of cigars from the case, makes a practice of holding it for an instant, by its side, and glancing at it admiringly, all before he hands it to the customer. He was weeks, he says, learning to hold the box at precisely the right angle. He calls this practice the "great silent drama of salesmanship," and he declares it is responsible for a great deal of his success.

It is interesting to see what happens in fund raising when it is put in the hands of a man with a keen sense of showmanship. James W. Young, noted advertising man, was once asked to take charge of a campaign for the annual Red Cross Roll Call in Kenyon County, Kentucky. Young ordered the biggest ledger that could be made—a really giant book—and had it dedicated at a public meeting, with all the leading citizens, clergymen, public officials, etc., present. The book was then displayed in a department store window with a pretty girl in Red Cross uniform who registered the names of people as they enrolled.

Publicity matter stated that when the enrollment was complete the book would go into the national archives of the Red Cross in Washington. When a man (or woman) enrolled, he got a button saying *My Name Is in the Book*, and householders got a window sticker with the same legend. The result? Kenyon County secured the highest percentage of enrollment that year of any county in the United States.

Showmanship has been defined as the art of attracting attention. It is vastly more than that. It is also the art of arousing interest and creating desire through the force of its emotional appeal. Lawyers have discovered, as Clarence Darrow demonstrated so often, that showmanship will often influence juries more effectively than hours of argument. Great revivalists are skilled in the arts of "theater," and so are great politicians.

Let me try further to illustrate the use of showmanship by an additional instance in a very ordinary business enterprise. Floyd L. Smith was the owner of a little restaurant in Seattle. He and his mother, who is his partner, observed that most people have a great yen for old-fashioned green-apple pie. They wondered how they could turn that fact into good account. They knew it was not enough merely to list apple pie on their menus, even if it was good yummy green-apple pie.

Meditating on this, they decided to make their restaurant known in Seattle as *The Home of the Green Apple Pie*, and this news they emblazoned on big signs for all to see. Inside the restaurant the hungry diner's eye is caught by the "Pie-O-Graph," a huge wall chart that records up-to-the-minute figures on the number of pies the restaurant has baked since the opening day in 1920—more than 1,800,000 currently, at the rate of two green-apple pies every sixty seconds.

When Jimmie H. Davis, governor of Louisiana, went stumping for votes, he ran on a platform of peace and harmony. "There were eleven of us youngsters," the governor explains, "and in a family that big you either have peace and harmony, or a full-fledged riot. We all grew up knowing the value of getting along with the other fellow."

Showmanship played a great part in putting over Jimmie's platform with the voters. He didn't argue the merits of peace and harmony. Saying as little as possible, he sang to them to the music of his own string band. "Ah don't want bickering and confusion," said the governor. "Ah want everybody happy."

Lest you think Jimmie's showmanship is an accident, the thoughtless antics of a hillbilly, let it be known that he is not only an ex-movie actor but also an ex-professor of history and social science, having taught at Louisiana's Dodd College. He knows what he is doing.

Bear in mind always that showmanship isn't "show*off*manship." Flagpole sitting, airplane marriages, walkathons and such stunts may attract attention, but they have no relationship to influencing people to think favorably of you and to do what you want them to do.

13
Putting Others on Your Team

When Dr. Henry Thomas wrote an interesting history of mankind a few years ago, he told the story of the world in terms of its leaders. He selected a small group of men and women whose lives had contributed to the onward march of civilization. These leaders ranged all the way from the wild-eyed Hebrew prophet Moses to mild-mannered Gandhi. They included leaders of thought, of politics, of religion, of governments, of military machines. The one thing these leaders had in common was the secret of leadership. Without exception they were men and women of imagination.

No matter where you find a leader even to this day, whether it is in business or in politics, in school activities or in the church, in small neighborhood affairs or in international cartels, there you will find a person of extraordinary imagination. Imagination is the one concomitant of leadership the world over.

It follows therefore that if you aspire to leadership in any activity (and almost every normal person does want to be a leader), the one quality you must have and apply is the imagination of leadership.

Let us take a look at some of these world leaders Dr. Thomas selected and see if we can find the thread of imagination running through the lives of all of them, different as all were in their thoughts, in their actions, in their careers.

He started the story by telling the achievements of Moses, a man whose imagination enabled him to lead his people out of subjugation and on to the plateau of freedom and independence.

Another ancient prophet was Jeremiah, leader of the world's thought. His powerful imagination pictured a world without incessant warfare. In creating such a world he was not successful, but his traits of leadership won him followers without number. And the Greek Pericles had a similar imagination, picturing a society in which all men would live as brothers—a true democracy. There followed Plato, that imaginative Greek scholar who pictured a better world. Alexander the Great had imagination, but it was attuned to different ends. To conquer the world was his dream—as it was the dream of Julius Caesar. All had imagination, you see.

And the same thing runs through all leaders of history, for all were men of vast imagination: Jesus Christ, with his conception of a new kind of religion; Charlemagne, imagining himself retrieving the Holy Grail; John Ball, leading with Wat Tyler the peasant's rebellion of 1381; Joan of Arc, savior of France; Martin Luther, with his high ideals of religious freedom; Spinoza, whose only desire was complete intellectual freedom; Napoleon, with his imaginings of conquest; Karl Marx, prophet of political freedom; Abraham Lincoln, whose desire was social equality; down to little Gandhi, whose dream was to see his own country free.

Without exception these men were men of vast imagination. They had in their power the ability to stir other men to action— and putting other men on your team is one of the most important factors in establishing yourself as a leader.

Always these men, by the very words they used, excited the imagination of others and made them willing followers, to the grave if necessary. Take Napoleon as an example of this.

With nothing to offer his armies except the opportunity of dying on far-flung battle fronts, Napoleon, by the images he was able to stir in the minds of his followers, made them eager to sacrifice themselves for him. Consider some of his utterances as examples of the use of words to stir imagination. Before he invaded Italy, he said to his armies, "We will levy twenty million francs on the Italians." Later, "I will lead you to the most fertile plains in the world. There you will find honor, glory, riches." In Egypt he declared, "Soldiers, from the tops of these pyramids forty centuries look down upon you."

Wherever you find leadership you will find some of the same kind of genius Napoleon had—the genius of stirring the imagination of others so that they will trust the leader and follow him wherever he leads.

What is this genius? To be extremely practical, can you master some of the principles of these leaders so that you in your own way and in your own field can put others on your team? You certainly can.

Let us see what these leaders have that makes them leaders.

The first thing the leader has is the ability to work with others. This in itself takes imagination. As I (Roth) told you in Chapter Eight, your whole success is going to be determined by how well you understand others and how well you make them understand you. Even a follower, as I pointed out there, has to keep step with others.

The leader has to understand people and keep step with them even more, for it is the leader who establishes the tempo of these steps. If you can handle people and can get them to work with you, you have the prime quality of leadership. "I will pay more for the ability to handle people than for any other ability," remarked John D. Rockefeller when he was asked what he looked for in other men.

All right. The second quality which the leader has to have is the ability to develop other men into leaders. He must be able to select, train, inspire other leaders. The history of every successful business is the history of one man who was able to surround himself with other men who had the qualities of leadership. You can see from this that leadership is an unselfish enterprise. It takes considerable imagination to look at a young man and sense in him leadership qualities that can be brought out.

Let me tell you about three great American leaders whose careers exemplify what I am explaining here.

Take Andrew Carnegie. No other American business genius ever created more leaders than Carnegie. When he was starting his steel empire, he surrounded himself with young men in whom he saw potentialities for leadership. While they were yet young, he invested these men with responsibility. He also gave each the opportunity for becoming rich. Carnegie is still referred to as "the man who made a thousand millionaires."

He was a man, don't you see, who had the imagination to perceive in other men qualities that would make leaders of them. And because he surrounded himself with men of leadership caliber, he built his own industrial empire to gigantic size.

The second man whose career I should like you to review was one of these young Carnegie leaders—Charles M. Schwab. Few business leaders have had the attractiveness of Charlie Schwab. Whatever he touched, he touched with the genius of his leadership. He had the imagination to see what others wanted, and he gave it to them. He in his turn made leaders of some of his younger associates.

The third man whose career in leadership points up the importance of imagination is John H. Patterson, the genius who created the cash register dynasty. With the exception only of Carnegie, no other man has created so many business leaders as Patterson. Even to this day the heads of some of America's largest corporations refer to themselves as "Patterson men," men trained in leadership by this able early business leader. One such man is Thomas J. Watson, fabulous head of International Business Machines.

How is it that some men are able to develop men around them and bring out the best in these men, while others are surrounded always by men of mediocre caliber and are usually in trouble with their associates?

If we can answer that question we can come close to finding one of the prime qualities of leadership. And I believe we can answer it. I should like to answer it by telling you about a friend who hasn't any of the qualities of leadership. For twenty years this man has tried to establish a small business in the graphic arts field, but he has had more failure and frustration than success. I do not believe any man has ever been associated with my friend for longer than three to six months. Then he and his associate quarrel, and split up. He then tries someone else, always with the same result.

Each time he selects a new man for a position with his firm, he tells me enthusiastically, "At last I've found the man I have been looking for. This time I know I have the right man." And then at the end of a few months the same old story—the unpleasant words, the misunderstanding, the severance of relations.

The only trouble with my friend is that he lacks the first quality of putting men on his team—and that lack is going to keep him forever from becoming a leader.

What quality is it? Men like Carnegie, Patterson, Schwab, Watson are what one man refers to as "goodfinders." They look for good in men, not bad. And because there is more good in all men than bad, leaders who look for good succeed in finding it. They thus encourage the men in whom they find it to work hard, to think for themselves, to develop latent abilities. Presently another capable executive emerges. But my unwise friend looks, not for good, but for bad. He is a fault-finder. And he likewise finds what he looks for—plenty to criticize in his employees. I am sure that if my friend the printer would just do a right-about-face in his thinking on this one point, he could build a successful business, for he is not dumb. But he does have one serious blind spot.

There used to be this conception of a leader: that he was a man who went around with a stern face, shouting orders to others, browbeating them, making himself detested—the old slave-driver conception, you know. The actual character of the leaders I have mentioned thus far and will mention presently belies this conception entirely.

When they were carrying the tremendous responsibility of operating the Carnegie Steel Company, the directors of that corporation, most of them young men under forty, were gay and lighthearted even during directors' meetings. There was none of that stern, intense fanaticism that used to be associated with leadership.

Once when a stockholder complained that there was entirely too much levity in the directors' meetings of the Carnegie company, Andrew Carnegie himself answered the letter. "I appreciate your interest in our management," said he. "Our company made a net profit last year of 20 per cent. If you can show me that being stern and sour-faced in our directors' meetings will increase profits, I will gladly substitute a stern and sour-faced board. But unless you can show me that, I believe we will continue just as we are."

As an example of a man who was a "goodfinder" rather than a faultfinder, and to bring out a little further the importance of this basic conception of leadership, consider the career and deportment of Henry P. Davison. As a Morgan partner, Mr. Davison had a large responsibility to carry. He could easily have taken himself so seriously that he would have made himself hated by everyone. What did he do? He became one of the kindest, gentlest, most considerate of men, always eager to look for what was good. He never found fault. Whenever someone went to Henry Davison with a proposition and asked his advice about it, instead of finding fault and looking for flaws, he looked for the good points, and actually found more good in the proposition to tell you about than the person himself had been able to find in it.

It takes imagination to see yourself in the proper relationship with others, to look for good instead of bad, to see that cooperation is essential to leading others. Every, leader has that kind of imagination.

He has with it certain specific qualities a leader must have, but these are without much value if a man lacks the fundamental imagination I have just discussed.

What are these specific qualities of leadership? Charles C. Stech, himself a business leader, recently declared that there are ten basic traits of leadership and that "successful leaders have these ten abundantly."

First Mr. Stech puts good judgment—the ability to make decisions on the basis of facts instead of emotion. "It surpasses all other qualities," he says. Next he puts the ability to plan—to use imagination to see ahead. Third comes justness, fairness in dealing with everyone. "These are the A B C of leadership," in Mr. Stech's opinion. "Men who possess these traits and little else will make leaders, though of course they should have much else."

They should also have open-mindedness. They should have initiative. They should have decisiveness. They should have enthusiasm. They should have ingenuity—that is, a lively imagination. And finally they should have resourcefulness, the ability to meet emergencies promptly.

I haven't mentioned another prime quality of leadership yet, but it is time to bring that into the picture now. It may be that this of all qualities is the most important, the only indispensable quality in anyone who aspires to lead. The name of this quality is courage.

A leader is a man who can keep going, in the face of every discouragement, a little longer than anyone else believes it is sensible to keep going. A leader is a man who can face disaster and still keep his faith in himself. A leader is a man who can go clear to the end of the road

And all leaders have to have such courage, for it is easy to become a leader—but difficult to remain one. You see, the routine of leadership is pretty well standardized. By distinguishing himself in some way, a man becomes a leader. Then everyone cheers. Friends send him congratulatory notes, and he is on the high road to popularity and fame. This is the starting point of most careers.

But then reverses come. The followers become disgruntled and desert. The unfaithful go to other leaders. Associates begin to lie down on the job. A spirit of dissension springs up. Factions are formed. The leader has to face the realities of leadership.

If he has the true quality of leadership, he sees conditions through, regardless of how bitter they may be, but if he lacks this quality he falters—and when he falters he is lost.

The true quality of leadership I am citing here, the quality that gives the leader the ability to see himself through every crisis— you know what it is, don't you? It is imagination. For if a man has imagination, he can easily see beyond the dark and hazardous present: he can see farther than the followers, see the time when his cause will be strong and he will be in command. Those less gifted with imagination see only the direful present. They are not leaders because they do not have the imagination of leadership. Unless they can acquire it, they can never be leaders.

A young woman of considerable ability started a business not long ago, and, after a very propitious start, ran into hard going. She called me just yesterday to ask me what she should do to keep from worrying about her business. As a matter of fact, she hasn't much to worry about—just a temporary setback such as every business has. But to her it spells curtains.

In a situation like hers, as I explained to her, a leader never falters. A leader sees beyond the temporary stringencies, and has imagination enough to see that these things all pass if the leader has courage enough, patience enough, faith enough in his own destiny to see any situation through. A leader has the kind of imagination recommended by Ralph Waldo Emerson when he said: "A man is to carry himself in the face of all opposition as if everything else in the world were titular and ephemeral but himself."

Can this prime quality of leadership, the quality of courage, which, incidentally, attracts others more than any other single quality and holds them, be acquired or is it inborn? I am quite sure it is an acquired characteristic. The fact is that few children have courage. Children run from disaster, and it is only after years of patient training at school, at home, in contact with others, that they develop the courage to face unpleasant situations and cope with them.

One student of leadership noticed an interesting thing about it. He noticed that leaders are usually men and women of middle age or even older before they attain their full stature of leadership. He wondered why. It occurred to him that leadership is a process of growth, and he traced the careers of leaders and found that little by little, one step at a time, the imagination of leadership is acquired. It is acquired by countless little acts of leadership and courage.

Where does all this discussion of the value of imagination in leadership and the necessity for courage lead you in your own desire to become a leader?

It leads you simply to this fact, that if you wish to get others to play on your team, you have to develop in your life the qualities that attract and hold others—the qualities I have been discussing for you here. And you develop those qualities just as you develop all other qualities, by application and practice.

One wise father I know has developed leadership in his son far beyond the son's age. He did it by following the path I am going to recommend to you. Even when the boy was small, the father encouraged him to assert himself in leadership—to be the captain of the ball team, the best swimmer in the neighborhood, things like that, you know, little things in themselves, but big in developing the character of a boy who would some day lead in bigger things. He nurtured the boy through high school and college, insisting that he learn how to understand and cooperate with others and take an active part in all group activities.

Once out of college, the boy went into business, and has become immensely successful. During the war he made a distinguished record for himself, solely, I am convinced, because he had learned from childhood what it takes to get others to want to be on your team.

As to specific suggestions for acquiring leadership, consider these:

First, wherever you are, assume a position of leadership.

It may be that you are not now a leader in anything, but there are numerous places where leadership is badly wanted. I am thinking particularly of church and civic and organization affairs. Here anyone who wishes to assume responsibility can find an opportunity to assume it. There isn't any better place for you to learn the track of leadership than right there. Accept the chairmanship of a committee, head a drive to raise funds, or do anything to get more practice in putting others on your team.

Second, learn more about the art of pleasing others and winning confidence.

Whatever else you say about leaders, you have to say that they have the art of attracting others. They have what is vaguely referred to as personality, which simply means that in them others see (here is imagination at work again) qualities that attract. Their secret is one that has already been mentioned—an interest in the other person.

A person who is doomed to be a follower will not have enough imagination to see that an unselfish interest in the other person attracts, while a selfish interest in oneself repels. Leaders who put others on their team take an interest in the other person and, by using imagination, see things through that person's eyes. That takes practice and training also.

Third, start looking for good in ideas that are brought to you rather than bad.

If leaders are "good-finders," not faultfinders, and you want to become a leader, you want to have the ability to find good in

others, and the sooner you start acquiring it the better. It is perhaps the hardest of all abilities to acquire and the last which most
persons do acquire, but if you want to be a leader, it seems to me
you can start looking for the positive qualities in others, rather
than the negative. As you develop the ability to see good qualities
and potentialities in others, you will acquire the traits which the
leaders all have.

14
No Idea Is Too Small to Win

In 1933, a man named J. L. Persons was seventy years old, broke, and out of a job. There was a depression on. His plight seemed hopeless. Anyone could have told him that. All he had in his favor was many years' experience as a shoe salesman—and an idea.

To see the power of imagination, look at Mr. Persons' subsequent history. Before he died, at the age of eighty-three, he was earning $10,000 a year. He had built up the largest call trade among the women of his city; nearly 3,000 women insisted on buying their shoes from Mr. Persons.

What was the idea that worked the near miracle in this old man's life? The simplest idea you could imagine: he merely gave his customers more personal attention than other shoe salesmen gave them. That took imagination.

This is the way his system worked. Suppose you are a woman and have found your way into the store where this genial, white-haired old gentleman waits on you. He does his best to serve you, and, whether you buy or not, he thanks you for coming in. (Gratitude always wins friends.) You like him for his graciousness. Before you leave he asks you if you would mind giving him the names of three of your friends— "just so I can give them the same kind of service you have told me you enjoyed, Mrs. Estabrook."

Since we all like to be important to our friends, you gave Mr. Persons the names of three of yours, as a matter of course, gave the names gladly. It pleased you to be asked for them. To each of these three women Mr. Persons sends a personal letter; a friendly, sincere, informal letter, inviting each to come in whenever she needs shoes. One woman in three, as a matter of cold statistics, can be depended upon to accept the invitation.

When she comes in, she receives the same gracious treatment, the same routine of attention. She responds by giving the names of three of her friends. They also receive letters. They also become Persons' customers and friends.

You see, Mr. Persons succeeded because he had imagination enough to see that if he could occupy the center of an ever-widening circle of customers, he couldn't help making sales.

A good many people believe that you have to have a revolutionary idea to make more money. They fail to realize that even the simplest of ideas, provided they are sound and are put to work, can make you more successful at whatever job you do—and might even make you rich.

As an example of a man who took a simple idea and became wealthy from following it, consider a fire insurance man who was forced to move from Iowa to Denver, Colorado, at the age of fifty on account of the illness of his wife. No city is easy to establish a fire insurance business in, especially when one is fifty years old and a stranger—and it was freely predicted that this man would have rough going. In less than ten years he had built up one of the largest agencies in the city and had become wealthy. Imagination did it.

This man's big idea was that if you would keep in constant touch with your prospects and customers, you couldn't help selling them their insurance. His imaginative way of keeping in touch consisted of simple, one-line letters, written in longhand, which he sent out on the first day of every month.

Largely as the result of these letters, he established himself in jig time. The letters appealed to the imagination of the men who received them. You might not think much of what the letters said, because they do sound like "old home week." You could write better letters yourself.

This is the way some of them ran. In January he wrote, "May your every endeavor this year be successful." In February, "I appreciate your confidence in me." April: "May the Easter Season bring you an abundance of good wishes." June: "Many, many thanks for your business." September: "We are grateful to you for our pleasant relations." November: "May you have many good things to be thankful for." December: "We wish you many joys this Christmas season."

Imagination is so powerful that it can invest even the simplest acts with miracles. Consider a young cigar salesman who believed firmly in the imaginative value of trifles. He spent months learning the best way to hand a customer a cigar—a detail so small other cigar salesmen consider it unimportant. It was important enough in this young salesman's life, however, to make him the head of a chain of cigar stores by the time he was forty. By handing a cigar to the customer in the right way, exactly the right way, he increased his average sale from two cigars to three—a net sales gain of 50 per cent. This is enough of a margin to make any business rich.

Another merchant, operating a small grocery store in a crossroads town in the South, used his imagination to win the gratitude—and business—of the mothers of the town. Where is there a mother who hasn't had the experience of sending a child to the store and having the child lose all or part of the change? The grocer perceived that if he could eliminate this loss he would win good will. It was easy. He did the obvious thing, which is usually the right thing: he wrapped the change in a small piece of paper. Result: good will and friendship and increased loyalty and patronage for his store.

A woman operator of a small fruit farm in Oregon discovered imagination indispensable in building the business of her roadside fruit stand. Along her stretch of highway were a dozen fruit stands, yet her fruit was all sold out by three o'clock, while the fruit on the other stands often spoiled for want of buyers. Why was she so successful? A curious customer decided to learn the reason. He found that it was the result of using imagination. What the successful woman did was use the age-old (but still popular) device of giving her customers more than they expected.

When she weighed or counted out the fruit, she would throw in an extra apple or pear "for good measure and friendship," she would smilingly explain. That show of generosity, which cost practically nothing in comparison with the results it yielded, made such a hit with customers that they told their friends. She became known as "the good-measure lady." Her business expanded greatly, while other stands went broke. Imagination to see what people want did the trick again, don't you see?

In the field of personal salesmanship, imagination applied to little things also works wonders, and any salesman who will invest his talk with imagination can accomplish great success. One salesman, by adding imagination to his otherwise commonplace sales talk, made 1,200,000 sales in a three-year period. He gave the talk 60,000 times to groups of varying sizes, made 20 sales each time he gave the talk. There was no magic in the 232 ordinary words that comprised this talk—the magic was in the imagination that was applied to the talk.

This man (to show you how he operated) ascertained that by making his pauses five seconds long—long enough to let the words sink in—he could add 10 per cent to his effectiveness: in other words, he could gain two more customers each time he talked. When he assumed an air of mystery at the beginning of the talk, he could add ten dollars a day to sales. Smiling was so important, he discovered, that it was worth fifty dollars a day to him.

Speaking of smiles reminds me (Roth) that the use of smiles, which requires imagination, is one of the most profitable practices anyone can follow. Yet how few persons are imaginative enough to perceive this! A newspaper columnist, after a week's survey, reported to me that only 4 per cent of the people he met with on the street have smiles on their faces. A friend of mine, wishing to test the efficacy of smiles, made an interesting experiment. He walked fourteen city blocks, smiling as he walked one block, walking with a glum face the next block, smiling the next, and so on for fourteen blocks. What do you suppose he discovered?

"If I ever was a fugitive from justice and wanted to remain obscure," he told me, "I know all I would have to do—not smile. I was completely ignored when I didn't smile, but the minute I put a smile on my face, three persons out of five noticed me—and smiled, too."

This man's next step was to apply the smiles technique to his business of selling life insurance. He consciously smiled more when talking to prospects and clients. At the end of the third month he took his financial bearings and found that he had increased his income 25 per cent.

Take the application of imagination to the problem all of us have of making appointments, often with busy people who don't want to see us. A young chap in New York City discovered that he was being turned down three times out of five when he tried to see important men. It was time he did something about it.

He set his lively imagination to work and turned up with this idea: Ask for appointments for odd hours, times that others wouldn't think of. It worked. He would ask for an appointment for three-twelve, for example, or for three-fifty-three. This idea increased his ratio of appointments 75 per cent.

The same man (incidentally, he rose to a position high in business) used his imagination to outsell, outsmart competitors. He was the youngest, greenest man in the field. He didn't have a look-in. It occurred to him that if he didn't do something soon he'd be out of a job. He applied imagination to the problem and concluded, "If I can spend more time with my prospects, even if I am not so smart as some of the other boys, I'll get my share of the business."

His next step was to study the work habits of his prospects. Every trade has its traditions, you know. His had. One tradition is that it is foolish to make calls on Saturday mornings because buyers are too busy to see you. He flew in the face of this tradition, this youngster did: he made calls on Saturdays, got in to see buyers easily, made some gravy sales. Another tradition is concerned with making calls on rainy days: don't, it says, "because every buyer is despondent when it rains." This man worked hardest on rainy days. His imagination let him see that if other salesmen weren't working then, buyers would welcome a man who did. And that is the way it worked out.

Another man tied up imagination with nine simple words, and sold an expensive suit of armor to a collector after the collector had said he wasn't going to buy. The sale amounted to thousands of dollars. Nine imaginative words clinched it

After the collector had said he wasn't going to buy the armor, the imaginative salesman walked over to it, tapped it with his finger, quietly remarked, "Just think! Maybe Shakespeare's eyes rested on this armor."

Nine words. But they set a whole train of imaginative thoughts coursing through the buyer's mind. After a little pause, he said, "I have reconsidered my decision. I want that armor."

Perhaps the most effective use of imagination in winning what you want, and the easiest form to apply, is merely to use it in studying what the people you have to please are looking for in life.

If you can by this simple process of imagination project yourself into the other person's life, see what he wants, there isn't any question about your making good. One youngster I knew did this. After working for several years for a large packing firm, he went into business for himself. He bought a secondhand truck and a supply of meat. Many men do this, but more fail than succeed. Those who fail usually do so because they have no imagination.

That wasn't ever a fault of Johnny Slattery. Ideas he had by the score, and the chief idea of all was that if he could give the customer exactly what the customer wanted—in service, in attention, in adherence to detail, in product—he would do all right by himself.

So, he put himself in the other fellow's shoes—the customer's—and although he lived just five years after he started in business, he built up one of the outstanding wagon wholesale businesses in the country. Four years after Johnny's death, I happened to go over his territory and talked to some of his customers. I found them still remembering him, still wishing they could find someone else who would understand and serve them as well as Johnny did.

It wouldn't be hard for you, no matter what your job or occupation, to put yourself on a basis of imagination. Try it. Put imagination into everything you do. Watch results. These won't disappoint you; for the fact is that imagination is without doubt the greatest touchstone to success anyone has discovered—and there isn't any idea too small to be made big if it is invested with the proper imagination.

Let me tell you how one man did this. He was an actor before the war, and served for over two years in the merchant marine.

When he got out of the service, he floundered. In his old profession there was little he could do—and he knew nothing else. Here was a man with a problem. What did he do?

Here is the answer in Arthur King's own words: "I looked within myself for years. I took a piece of paper and wrote down as in a geometry problem all my abilities. Opposite them I wrote why they couldn't mean money for me.

"Finally, at the end of a very long list which included jingle writing, advertising layout, mail order, I remembered that I could make jewelry; not only make it, but design some very unusual jewelry. Here at last I had something—I hoped!"

That was the first step in imagination—getting an idea. But putting the idea over required even more of Arthur King's imagination. He had it to use for that purpose. He designed and sent out samples. These took hold. He began giving little one-man exhibitions. These attracted attention. All the time he was using his imagination boldly to conceive new designs—and even more boldly to put them across.

At present: "Just a little over three months from my original sample making, I am exhibiting in one art gallery here in New York City, have appeared as a guest celebrity on a radio program, and have a staff of four people working for me. I have taken a studio in Provincetown as well as in New York.

"A great many other things are on the fire for the near future—such as an exclusive showing in the second floor gallery of a large Chicago department store. All this is very encouraging to me."

Mr. King believes that there are many, many veterans in the plight he was in; he believes, and so do I, that not only veterans but everyone else, old and young, could get out of their plight just as he did, by employing their imagination to do the job!

15
IDEAS WIN FOR WOMEN

Are you thinking of launching a small business of your own? Perhaps a dress shop, or a rental library, or a little candy shop, or a modest tearoom, or a delicatessen?

Or, if not anything so crassly commercial, are you flirting with the notion of going it alone as an interior decorator, or an artist, or a landscape gardener, or what not?

If you are, your chance of success will be vastly greater if "something new has been added." Get yourself an idea, a new "angle"—figure out a way to be different, a way to give people a *plus* they are not getting now.

A good idea is, oftener than not, an asset more valuable than plenty of money in the bank.

Listen to this story about a young schoolteacher who quit her job, started a business of her own in downtown Denver, made a handsome profit the first week. And, confounding the experts, she has been going like a house afire ever since.

She had never been in business on her own before, and for capital all she had was $100 in cash and $1,700 in war bonds.

But she had one thing that was priceless—a fat black notebook which you shall now hear about.

Ten years ago Mary Ann Fisher, barely out of her teens, dreamed of some day owning and operating a travel bureau. There was nothing else in the world she wanted to do so much. On a schoolteacher's pay she couldn't save much for the enterprise, and besides she spent every extra cent in traveling all over the United States, Mexico, and Canada.

Instead—and here's where that black book comes in—she saved *ideas*.

This book was her constant companion wherever she went. In it she jotted down ideas about how to run a travel bureau. From Montreal to Mexico City she would talk earnestly with porters, railway conductors, ticket agents, taxi drivers, bellhops, hotel clerks, bus drivers, airline stewardesses, travel agents, and literally hundreds of tourists. "How have you enjoyed your trip?" "Has anything gone wrong?" "How could your trip have been made easier, less bother, more fun?" She did that for ten years. She still does it.

She established friendly contacts, too, with hotel and resort managers, steamship officials, and other such dignitaries, a matter that couldn't have been too difficult for a young woman so gracious and altogether lovely to look at.

"Ideas were so precious to me," declares Miss Fisher, her eyes sparkling, "that I didn't want to lose a single one of them. It didn't take me long to see that, while traveling is great fun, it is also a great annoyance. There are so many disappointments when one travels—lack of hotel accommodations, poor service, indifference of ticket agents, ignorance of the best way to route a traveler, and so on. Why, I asked myself, can't travel be arranged so that there will be no petty irritations, no confusions, no discomforts, and, most important, no unexpected expenses? This last is the worst of all—dozens of items of extra cost one hasn't counted on."

Today—and this is the gospel truth—that dog-eared well-thumbed notebook of Miss Fisher's bulges with more than three hundred ideas about better travel service.

Are you thinking of going into business for yourself? Then listen to this. "Having all those ideas to draw on," explains Miss Fisher, "I started with definite plans and practices all mapped out. *From the first day on I haven't had a single hour of groping and bewilderment such as most persons have when they set out on a new enterprise.*"

She had some tough nuts to crack right off. On her first day a businessman threw this at her: "I have the damnedest family in the United States. Scattered like a covey of quail. Wife's in New York. Eldest boy in Miami. One of my daughters is in Bennington,

Vermont, in school. Teddy's at Culver. Gather 'em together in Chicago, and I'll meet them there and bring them home."

Well, it took two weeks and sixty dollars' worth of long-distance calls to make plane, train, and hotel reservations, but the intrepid Miss Fisher and her idea book did it. And that task began on her first day, mind you, before she had time to take off her hat.

In the midst of this bustle and hustle in walked a schoolteacher and her mother, greenhorn travelers, with a yen to see New England—a lot of it. For that little jaunt Miss Fisher had to make nearly one hundred reservations—plane, train, bus, hotel, resort, camp—and prepare an itinerary seven pages long. Everything went off without a hitch; the trip was a huge success.

Miss Fisher's most popular idea is what she calls her One Phone Call Service. For example, a businessman phones that he wants to fly to Seattle, fly from there to San Francisco for a two-day meeting, go from there to Los Angeles, where he will spend a week, and then stop at Palm Springs for a few days' rest on the way back. "Just one phone call to me," says Miss Fisher, "and he can forget it. I deliver to his desk his tickets, reservations, detailed instructions. He writes out a check covering everything, and that is all there is to it."

The delivery is made, by the way, by a youngster all dressed up in a natty blue uniform like a commander in the Navy. Businessmen hate to drop everything to pick up tickets. Johnny does it for them. Miss Fisher trained him in the best way to enter an office, how to address clients, and what to say and how to say it. Johnny has taken Denver by storm.

Another popular idea is Miss Fisher's Travel Library. A collector of travel books for years, she lends them to her clients without charge. With your transportation to Cuba you get a couple of books on the country. There is also the Mary Ann Fisher Travel Club, its membership the men and women who have traveled under her sponsorship, which meets once a month for a talkfest, a movie, refreshments— "and," smiles Miss Fisher, "a lot of boasting about the places we have seen. It is one of my Number One ideas."

Because she believes most folks like to see their names in print, Miss Fisher releases a story to the local papers whenever one of her clients takes a trip (with the client's approval, of course). Usually this gets into the society section, and another loyal booster is added to the roster.

Hotels are tipped off when a Fisher client is coming, and "you would be surprised at how he beams," declares Miss Fisher, "when the hotel manager exclaims, 'Why, Judge Whitford, how glad we are to see you! We have been expecting you.'" All Fisher clients, incidentally, are provided with a card of introduction to the hotel manager.

An idea which Miss Fisher calls "one of my pets" is her Trip-of-the-month Plan. She is busy on it now. "It will be," she says, "a week end for, oh, twenty-five to thirty dollars, and will give people a chance to go to some new place each month, without fuss or bother, every detail of the trip all planned. It will fill a long-felt need." Her low-cost "Package Tours" are already tremendously popular. For as little as seventy-five dollars she offers "not an ordinary trip where you are herded like a jury panel on its way to lunch, but a dignified tour with first-class accommodations."

The Fisher Five-year Vacation Plan—a "looking ahead" program—is a story by itself. So is her Specialized Tours Plan which provides especially arranged trips for different "interest groups"— fishermen, hunters, butterfly collectors, archeologists, skiers, camera fans, and so on. Then there is her plan, an arrangement with a Denver bank, for financing travel; her planned Gift Trips for birthday, graduation, wedding, and Christmas presents; her Special Attention Service for old people, invalids, and children; her Junior Travel Groups, made up of teen-agers, which are entertained once a month with travel movies, stories, and refreshments. "Some day," says Miss Fisher, "these youngsters will be my clients."

Miss Fisher today has a prosperous, ever-growing business. Twice she has had to move to larger quarters and her plans for expansion are breath-taking.

Maybe you'll find your idea in *specialization*. There is in Santa Fe a little dress shop called Pins and Needles. It specializes in peasant-type blouse-and-skirt costumes, made to the customer's order, and done in the spirit of the old Spanish Southwest. It serves a real need, both for residents and for visitors, Santa Fe being the romantic town that it is. There is no other shop like it in town; hence it is a unique business idea and stands out from the crowd.

It was an idea that gave Lily Dache her start. She began by buying for a hundred dollars a run-down, hole-in-the-wall millinery shop. She had no capital, no stock, no prestige. But she had imagination. When a woman came in for a hat and asked to see models, Miss Dache flew into a Gallic rage and said, "I wouldn't think of letting you wear a hat that someone else wears. I will design something special for you." With the two-dollar deposit she rushed out and bought material and cut and fitted that hat on the woman the next day. Ideas such as this made Lily Dache the spectacular success she is today.

There is the case of a girl named Jean who didn't even have the proverbial shoestring. Ousted from her job as a clerk and stenographer in a Washington insurance office, she was penniless. But she did have an idea, and she borrowed two hundred and fifty dollars to rent an office and start a business of her own. She knew there were many hard-pressed insurance agents, who, to keep down their costs, handled their own burdensome clerical work. Here clearly was a "slant." Agents flocked to her. Today Jean and her staff do the worrying and the paper work for more than 100 agents, while a score of others make her office their headquarters. An unfilled need, an idea that met it—how could she miss!

Inspiration is to be found in the story of Mary Imogene Shepherd. Watching her patrons sit under hot hair driers in the beauty salon of a Chicago department store gave her an idea. Why, she asked, isn't there a cream these women can rub on their faces as they sit here—a cream that will restore the natural oil these driers are stealing from their skins?

She began experimenting on a compensating cream at home. Meeting with no success, she followed a habit she had developed for solving problems she couldn't handle: she consulted her Bible. She opened it at the thirtieth chapter of Exodus, and her eye fell on: "This shall be an holy anointing oil. . . ." Reading on, she came to a formula for ointment and she decided to analyze it. That analysis gave her certain information she needed to continue her research— research that resulted in her finding just the recipe she sought.

Mrs. Shepherd's boss, Mr. Elmer Stevens, president of Charles A. Stevens and Brothers, bought an experimental quantity of the new oil for the store's beauty shop. Patrons liked the product and began insisting on some to take home. Mrs. Shepherd's imagination was equal to the occasion. She began the manufacture of her magic cream, and now sells it over cosmetic counters from Maine to Mexico.

Speaking of cosmetics and such things, it was Miss Edna Murphy who pioneered teaching women to prevent underarm odor. Her father, a surgeon, bothered by perspiration of his hands in the operating room, concocted a formula to forestall it. Miss Murphy, her imagination caught by the product, pondered for a long time on how her father's formula could be put to wide general use. Finally she hit upon an idea: Why not sell the new mixture to stop underarm odor? Beginning with a few dollars of capital, Miss Murphy bottled the product in her kitchen and peddled it, going from door to door. Thus Odo-ro-no was born—and it rode to success on the power of an idea.

But perhaps you don't want a shop, product, or business undertaking of your own but seek to capitalize on some special talent you may possess. Well, there is the case of Mrs. Pansy Stockton, of Santa Fe, who wasn't satisfied with painting in the conventional style. Years ago she realized that if she could produce something different—if she could think up an original art treatment—her work would stand out and attract attention.

Pansy Stockton pushed her imagination hard and came up with a brand new idea—Sun-Paintings, a name of her own coining. She produces Sun-Paintings without oils or water colors or crayons of any kind. She "paints" with the vegetable materials of nature: dried leaves, grasses, bits of bark, moss, lichens, twigs, roots, flowers, even weeds. These bits of flora, gathered in the fields and forests, are put together in the form of a mosaic and then pasted on a piece of paper board. The effect is beautiful and spectacular.

Pansy Stockton's idea has won her fame and a comfortable income. Her Sun-Paintings are hung in Washington, Paris, and London, and are everywhere in demand.

Here is an idea suggested by a bachelor friend of mine. "I only wish," he says, "that some imaginative woman would establish a service shop for us poor victims of bachelorhood—a place we could go to have our shirts mended and buttons sewed on; our socks darned; our neckties cleaned and pressed; our parties planned and managed (including the making of the hors d'oeuvres and punch, and the planning of the table setting, flower arrangement, and favors for the ladies), and what not." Offering the services of an Emily Post, cook, seamstress, and laundress, the enterprising woman who accepts this challenge might name her shop Bachelor's Paradise with out seeming to exaggerate.

But you don't have to start a business, and you need not be a talented artist, to make ideas work for you. No job is so commonplace that an employee can't get ahead by thinking up better ways of doing things.

There's Josephine Burns Kelly, a hatcheck girl in Chicago's popular Wrigley Building Restaurant.

"My gracious," Josie exclaimed on her first day, "here's a coat with two buttons missing, here's another with a rip in the lining, and here's another . . . !" So Josie got herself a little workbasket full of needles, buttons, darning cotton, corsage pins—as well as aspirin for headache sufferers—and ever since she has been making repairs free of charge. Besides, patrons are never irritated by the loss of hatchecks, because Josie never issues them: she always knows which article of clothing or package belongs to which customer. "Buttons have not only supported me," says Josie, "but they sent my boy through military school."

Perhaps you need not look outside your own home for the idea that will bring success. One woman, the proprietor of a prosperous baking business in Pennsylvania, began in a very small way by selling her own special kind of cookies and doughnuts right out of her kitchen. A Chicago woman, famous among her friends for her homemade salad dressing, put it up in bottles, persuaded a few stores to sell it, and now she has a little business that gives her a comfortable living. Still another woman serves a select clientele of forty or fifty families, as well as a half dozen jewelry stores. She is an expert polisher of silver. She uses a polish and a technique of her own contriving, and the luster she gets is beautiful. During these days of servant shortage she and two assistants are constantly in demand.

Often what seems at the time a little idea leads to big results. Susan Stavers, for example, once served some tapioca pudding to a Boston sailor. He wouldn't eat it because it was lumpy. So was all tapioca at that time. She ground a batch before cooking it. It worked: there were no lumps when it was cooked. When the sailor came to the restaurant again she persuaded him to try the lumpless tapioca. He did—and raved about it. Not only did the grinding eliminate the lumps; it led to quicker cooking. She named the powder "Minute Tapioca" and became famous.

Imagination—for men or for women—is the greatest single force in business.

16
KEEPING A STEP AHEAD OF THE PARADE

They celebrated the one hundredth birthday of a remarkable American not so long ago. He is Henry C. Lytton, one of the great merchant princes of Chicago. Sensing the interest in a man who at the age of a hundred could remain active in business and come to his office every day, the publicity department of the store which Mr. Lytton founded made much of his birthday. They sent interviews with the old gentleman to all the papers. Magazines carried stories about Henry Lytton. Radio stations dedicated programs to him. There was newspaper, outdoor, direct-mail advertising. His birthday was celebrated in the traditional manner.

Throughout all these activities Mr. Lytton, who is a realist, was patient and understanding. But toward the end he became a little bit annoyed that they should take up so much time celebrating, so he said to one of his associates, "Let's get this over with as soon as possible. I have some new ideas I want to talk to you about."

There, it seems to me (Roth), you have the secret of a man who at the age of one hundred is the head of a business that is looking forward, not backward, and one that is still a step ahead of the parade.

The reason why Mr. Lytton has attained so much, kept himself so young, is that he has always used his imagination. Even at the age of a hundred, he's thinking of tomorrow. He has ideas!

In the career of that man there is a story which more businessmen ought to practice. The rule is that if you want to keep a step ahead of the parade you have to keep a step ahead of everyone else in the full use of your imagination.

When publisher Frank A. Munsey died, he left an estate of more than $20,000,000. Practically every dollar in that estate came to Frank Munsey because, throughout his long and active and eager life, he was a man who used his imagination tirelessly to do what I am recommending here for you—he kept a step ahead of the parade.

In one of the national magazines a former editor on one of the Munsey papers, Stanley Walker, summed up Mr. Munsey's amazing career as a publisher by saying, "He got ahead by his brash ambition, by hard work—but mostly by a lively imagination."

Then Mr. Walker explained that Munsey, even as an elderly man and not always well, was just a step ahead of his associates, most of whom were picked because they were "idea men." He was always projecting his ideas into the future, five years into the future, ten years, even twenty years into the future. He was always thinking ahead. Those with whom he surrounded himself—and they were the highest paid and most talented men in their line—had to pant mentally to keep up with Frank Munsey; his mind was so active, his imagination so lively.

If you take the story of any successful man or any successful business that has managed to keep going year after year, you are apt to find the use of imagination like that of Frank Munsey—imagination to keep ahead of the parade—one of the prime reasons for continued success.

One wholesaler explained to a reporter that the only reason his century-old firm had been able to keep in the vanguard while many of its contemporaries went into bankruptcy was that the firm had a slogan: *Imagination and hard work will accomplish wonders.*

"There you have the real reason why we haven't slipped," the wholesaler explained. "We use our imagination every day, thinking ahead of where we will be and what we will be doing five, ten years hence. Then we go out and work hard to carry out our plans. It's all so simple, don't you see?"

It is simple. It is so simple that many organizations overlook the necessity for putting imagination to work in order to keep ahead of the parade. I could cite a dozen instances offhand of businesses that slipped backward because someone in charge didn't see any necessity for keeping ahead of the parade.

One large hardware store I know was firmly entrenched in its market twenty years ago. Its position was enviable: it served an empire virtually without competition. It should still be out ahead of the parade. But it slipped. Those at the head of the business thought they could operate without thinking ahead. They tried. The business went into receivership ten years ago. A lumber firm I knew intimately had the same experience, and the reason for its demise was the same—lack of projected imagination.

To show you what a man of projected imagination can do, however, with a business in keeping it ahead I want to tell you about a friend named John H. Jacobs. When John took over the family business he was only twenty-eight, the business was exactly twice his age—but as old as Methuselah in its methods and thinking. It was rapidly reaching the point where something drastic would have to be done or it would start going downhill fast.

The story of what John Jacobs did with the old confectionery company shows what can be done to keep ahead of the parade.

"When my uncle died and I was elected president of the firm," he told me recently, "it didn't take long to put my finger on the sorest spot in the picture.

"Our trouble was that we were looking backward, with all our might, instead of forward. Prior to 1928 the business had been very successful. The management figured the way to keep it successful was to do business in the way it was done in 1928.

"I took over in 1940. My first job was to reorganize my thinking and the thinking of my associates. I had to do this before I attempted any changes. Our thinking wasn't modern; even mine wasn't. Until we got our thinking on the modern plane our service couldn't be modern."

During the six years that he has been president of the firm, Mr. Jacobs instituted numerous changes—all for the purpose of modernizing the business, its services, and its products.

At first he met with a great deal of resistance from those whose thinking, as he puts it, "was still in 1928 mental channels." He met this opposition with good nature but firmness, for he was the boss

and insisted his ideas be carried out. There were some resigna-
tions. There was no more grumbling. But he stuck by his guns, and,
gradually, he won over his most obdurate associates to his way of
thinking.

But he wasn't through when he modernized the functioning and
the methods and the procedures of the business. That was only the
first step. His next step was to guarantee that the firm would always keep ahead of the parade. That was when he started making
plans *twenty years in advance.*

"Today every key employee of this organization is thinking in
terms of 1966," he told me recently. "None of us can know exactly
what conditions then will be like, for that's expecting too much
projection for anyone. But we do know this, that no matter what
conditions are, we will be ready for them—our thinking is slanted
toward that future date."

That is what I call keeping a step ahead of the parade, using
your imagination to project yourself so far ahead that no competition can keep up with you. Jacobs showed me some of his plans for
next year, for two years from now, for five years hence, for ten years
hence. He's ready for the future. You can't tell me that a business
which is operated on that basis is going to have to worry much
about competition or the ravages of dry rot.

Another man I know has met this matter of keeping ahead of
the parade realistically, also. He operates a music store. A few years
ago he took in a youngster who gave promise of becoming an asset
to the firm. At the end of the third year, however, the young man
felt he had served his apprenticeship. He was ready to spread his
own wings; so he announced he was going to strike out for himself.

"I'm going to take your customers away from you," he announced to his erstwhile employer. "I know who they are. I know
your methods. You won't be in business five years from now."

"I don't believe you can do that to us, Dave," the merchant declared. "It's true that you are a very popular, pleasing young man.
True also it is that you have had access to our records and customers. But there's one thing you don't have—and can't get."

"What's that?" the young man asked.

"You don't have a copy of my mind. You can copy our business methods. You can send letters to our customers. You can do the things that we've taught you to do. But you can't know what plans I have for doing new things for my customers. You can't copy another man's mind or his imagination. So, Dave, I believe if anybody's out of business five years from now, it will be you. I think we will still be here."

And that's the way it turned out. The younger man, filled with youth and self-confidence and energy, felt that he could conquer the world. But the thing he didn't reckon with was change, new ideas, new slants and attacks. Although he rented a store in the same block as his old employer and imitated the business methods of the older firm, he couldn't cope with a vital imagination. Inside of three years he gave it up as a bad job.

It of course isn't vouchsafed to anyone to penetrate the future too far, but anyone who will keep a flexible mind can penetrate it far enough to keep ahead of the parade. One of the best examples of this that I know of is the story of a fight between two large mail-order houses for a certain market.

One of these firms was well established in the market and superciliously strong and arrogant about it, while the other had been trying for several years to get a foothold. The competition of the first firm was too much. It offered more—more service, better values. Then this valuable element of imagination was brought to bear. A new merchandise man entered the picture, took a look around him, and said, "All we have to do is to go our competitor one better. We'll offer service nobody else has ever offered. Let's see if we can put our imagination to work on this problem."

He put his to work. A few weeks later the community was startled by an announcement—the most astonishing development in mail-order merchandising. It was sensational. You telephoned your order in the morning. It was radioed to a city six hundred miles away that afternoon. Your merchandise came in that night by special plane. Next day it was delivered to your door. See what a hold on the imagination a merchandising routine of that kind has?

This one bold stroke of imagination offset the advantages of the competing firm, left that firm floundering, looking for an idea that would enable it to keep up with the parade.

The most encouraging thing about having a good imagination—and being willing to use it—is that you can offset almost any condition, meet any situation that arises, and come out on top in almost any kind of a scrap. That quality of imagination is an infallible aid to anyone who will use it. If you want to keep a step ahead of the parade so that you will always be able to do business, make money, win new customers and success, it isn't hard. In just a few suggestions I can give you the background you need for that.

First suggestion: *Develop an open-mindedness toward everything and everybody.*

Have no prejudices. One reason why some persons cannot use enough imagination to accomplish great things is that they are walled in tight by prejudices. Their imaginations haven't enough room to turn around in. Men and women who keep ahead of the parade, however, keep an open mind and take an interest in everything.

Second suggestion: *Keep abreast of changes that occur in your business or field.*

Whenever a change occurs, it means someone has used his imagination to discover a better way to do a thing. There isn't any reason why you shouldn't know what other imaginations are doing—because each change might suggest in your mind an improvement on the change. That is the reason for keeping up with the world.

The way to keep abreast of changes is, of course, to read more. As a class, businessmen are poor readers. The daily paper, a news magazine, preferably one with a lot of pictures—isn't that about the size of the reading of the average businessman you know? And he wonders why so many things take place that he knows nothing about until long afterward.

I think that a half hour of serious reading each day—not reading best sellers but matter that will acquaint you with the real thinkers of our day and other days—would do much toward giving a man the inspiration he needs to keep himself ahead of the parade.

"The trouble with reading such a man," wrote Elbert Hubbard of Edgar Saltus, a writer whom he admired, "is that he makes you want to pick up your pencil and begin writing yourself."

There are writers like that—writers who inspire you to think. You're lucky if you know who they are; luckier still if you don't know who they are, for think of the fun you will have in discovering them.

Read trade magazines and business books too, in addition to news magazines and magazines of general interest. In short, fill your mind with ideas, with the thoughts of other men, with the results of the imagination of other men—and then your own imagination will have the raw materials it needs to go to work for you.

Third suggestion: *Try to think ahead of your times.*

Mark Twain said that being a prophet was the easiest job in the world: all you had to do was stop thinking and start talking. But that isn't the kind of activity I am suggesting to you. You know what products or services your firm now supplies. What will both be like twenty-five years hence, fifty years hence? Do some thinking on that subject. You might turn up with some surprisingly interesting ideas. You never can tell.

Fourth suggestion: *Be prepared to fight for your new ideas.*

No new idea, regardless of its merit, ever succeeded without a tough, heartbreaking fight. I recollect reading about Sir Henry Bessemer, inventor of the steel-making process which still bears his name. Sir Henry was a brilliant engineer, inventor, and industrialist. He fairly bristled with ideas; not half-baked, wistful, dreamy ideas, but practical ideas that were years ahead of their time.

When he was quite young he discovered that having ideas was one thing; having them accepted was quite another. He started out with his first invention under his arm, his mind filled with the naive belief that the world would take him and his new ideas close to its bosom. Nothing of the kind. He was scoffed at for his new ideas. A less resolute man would have broken under the strain. That treatment only made Sir Henry Bessemer more determined.

It took him twenty-three years of solid, almost daily pounding to have one of his ideas adopted. It took him seven years to demonstrate the superiority of steel rails over the soft iron rails then in use.

In his latter years he recollected that not one of his hundred inventions that eventually became successful and universal was adopted without terrific battles.

Let me give you another example of a man who was ahead of the times and had to wait nine years for the acceptance of his idea. King C. Gillette was his name; the safety razor was his invention. Gillette, a salesman in quest of an idea, his imagination working overtime, was forty when he hit upon the idea of a razor with a replaceable blade. He thought his fortune was made.

But he was too far ahead of the parade and had to wait for the elephants to catch up. All he met when he tried to interest users in his safety razor was jibes or indifference. For nine long years he marched a step ahead of the world, this resolute ex-salesman with his "funny" ideas.

So don't expect too much of your ideas, especially if they are at variance with the accepted mode of the times. But keep on having your ideas, and keep on thinking ahead—it's the only way you can be sure of getting ahead.

Final suggestion: *Never be satisfied with things as they are.*

When H. G. Wells a number of years ago issued his famous book on the history of the world, he made an unforgettable statement. He said that there was only one unpardonable sin in nature. It was stagnation, standing still.

Wells proved that animals and races of men alike perished when they didn't find better ways of doing things. They couldn't stand still and be satisfied. They had to change, to evolve, to improve.

Part of my job for years has been to watch the progress or retrogression of business concerns, and one fact has always struck me vividly; whenever a firm starts going backward, you will find complacency somewhere. Someone in the organization says, "Here we have struck perfection. Let's keep on doing it this way from now on." And that man or that firm is due for some serious trouble.

If you will develop what Emerson calls "divine discontent," you will be safe; and only if you develop that will you be safe. Question everything you do, even the most cherished things. Ask yourself if there isn't a better way to do them. Let your imagination set to work in seeking out improvements. Don't stand still:

Keeping a step ahead of the parade isn't any more difficult than adopting and following the few suggestions I have given you here. But no man who keeps a step ahead of the parade will ever be in danger of being trampled—he'll always be out ahead where he will be safe.

Even if he lives to be a hundred years old as Henry C. Lytton did, he will be safe if he can say as Henry C. Lytton did on his hundredth birthday, "I have some new ideas I want to talk to you about."

That's the thing which keeps you out ahead of any parade—new ideas. It doesn't make any difference what kind of strange conditions may come, a man who is equipped with new ideas can meet them.

17
It Pays to Be Different

My (Woolf) good friend, Jean Dubois, an excellent photographer in Denver, said to me with a wistful sigh, "Oh, how I wish my business was unique! Every mother's son and his brother in Denver is a commercial photographer, and most of them are pretty good. If only I were in an enterprise that was really different from the other fellow's."

He has a point. So many new entrepreneurs risk their savings and hopes of success in crowded dog-eat-dog fields. Launching the usual lunch counter or repair shop in a town or neighborhood already overserved by a plethora of the usual lunch counters and repair shops, they are lucky indeed if they survive.

In this chapter are related the stories of a number of persons—men and women, young and old—who are doing well in small enterprises, some of which can be started with little or no capital, that because they are different stand out from the standard run-of-mine businesses.

The Worm Turns—Into Cash

When Frank O'Brien came back to Denver, after five years in the Army, he knew exactly what he was going to do. A cashier for the Denver Welfare Bureau before his enlistment, he and his mother had operated in their spare time a little "factory" in their backyard lot. It had earned them a little money and seemed destined to go places—until, just when he was needed most, Frank marched off to war.

Their business began as a hobby. The mother, Catherine by name, and Frank, her husband, and their brood of three sons and six daughters, were all ardent fishermen. Thinking it might be a good idea to raise their own bait, they dug a pit in their backyard lot, filled it with a mixture of mulch, compost, and several edible items such as alfalfa and soybean, and stocked it with five dollars' worth of earthworms. Thus pampered, the worms multiplied like rabbits.

Soon their worms were in demand by fellow fishermen. And now and then they would get an order from truck gardeners, farmers, horticulturists, and orchidists who wanted earthworms for organic gardening purposes. Everywhere, growers of plant life were belatedly becoming earthworm-conscious. Experiments in citrus groves had shown that a given area, earthworm-treated, had produced up to 60 per cent more fruit than untreated areas in the same groves. Of particular significance was a large order for earthworms from a health clinic. The worms were wanted for use in organic gardening to produce superior vegetables for patients suffering from certain degenerative diseases.

It began to appear that they had something bigger than a hobby, and Frank considered quitting his job. Then the war changed everything. Frank's going left Mother Catherine holding the bag. Father O'Brien, tolerantly amused by all this "earthworm nonsense," would have none of it; he would stick to his little business of job printing. Happily, mom held the bag magnificently, despite her fifty-seven years. Not only did she do spadework in the pits. Studying every book and pamphlet on the subject she could find, she made many experiments in the science of earthworm breeding. Frank was missed, and some days his mother and sisters worked as long as fifteen hours, but she was deeply contented: the business was growing, and growing so fast that the little backyard lot was no longer adequate. Frank had been sending her every cent he could spare from his army pay, and with this money, a little over four hundred dollars, she purchased a small lot adjoining their home. She installed cement-lined pits in the new lots and paid for them out of accumulated earnings.

Thus it was that when Frank came home from the war his mother had a small but going business waiting for him. At this time of writing Frank has been back in the business for nineteen months. In that time sales volume has more than quadrupled, and it keeps everybody (except father O'Brien) jumping. Frank's pretty wife, Mary Louise, gives her full time to correspondence, bookkeeping, etc. Three of Frank's sisters, all married, help regularly. Mother Catherine, who enjoys maintaining the fiction that she is retired, is the busiest of the lot; right now she is absorbed in a series of experiments aimed at producing bigger and better earthworms. Frank's brother Joe, also a veteran, helps out in his spare time and earns from twenty to twenty-five dollars a week to fatten his regular pay envelope as a telephone company installer. Hordes of children are employed daily in the summer to pick worms.

Of the goodly sums the business pays to six or seven members of the O'Brien family, Frank's share for 1948 will exceed five thousand dollars. He thinks that's pretty good, inasmuch as he nearly decided to be a Denver policeman, instead of an earthworm farmer, when he first came back from overseas.

Frank went after the bait market first. He canvassed the whole Denver area, a popular fishing region, and stocked his worms in hundreds of sporting goods and hardware stores, filling stations, and lakeside hot-dog stands. This was quick easy business that provided him with needed money for further expansion. A few inexpensive ads in *Organic Gardening*, a magazine devoted entirely to compost farming, brought him a flood of inquiries and orders. Beyond this his business had been built up largely by favorable word-of-mouth advertising. Unsolicited orders have come to him from Canada, Australia, South Africa, England, Alaska, New Zealand, Canal Zone, and Hawaii. Since the beginning of the business, Frank estimates he has not spent more than fourteen hundred dollars for advertising and promotion—and this sum has come out of earnings.

How big is the potential in the earthworm business? Frank doesn't know, but he is sure it is tremendous. He believes that as yet the market has hardly been scratched. In face of a growing interest in the earthworm for organic-gardening purposes, the earthworm population of America is decreasing. It is decreasing because farmers have been scraping away the nation's topsoil for genera-tions, leaving the worms no protection against sudden freezes. Frank believes that the three million earthworms he sold in 1947 are only a tiny fraction of the potential.

"I think there is plenty of room for many more earthworm hatcheries," declares Frank. "One important advantage is the fact that so little capital is required to start. The only equipment that is needed are a few shovels, a wheelbarrow, and some pails and boxes. The pits do not need to be lined with cement; secondhand lumber will do almost as well. The operator need not invest in real estate; a long-term lease on an empty lot will serve his purposes. If he is willing to dig his own pits, his labor cost will be nothing. His total initial investment should not exceed five hundred dol-lars. But of course he should have some means of supporting him-self during the early development period of three or four months."

Frank adds one final word of advice: "I think I should say that the earthworm business is no easy road to riches. We work hard and our hours are often long. But since I am running my own busi-ness I do not mind. I am a contented man.

"But I shouldn't say my own business. It's mom's too, and she is the most contented woman in the world."

Station Wagon Rejuvenation

There is a man in Los Angeles, Conrad Schatte, who is running a unique and profitable enterprise that may be just the business idea you have been looking for.

Con says that any fellow who has a knack with tools and a paint-brush and is handy around cars, can duplicate his success. Not that Con is so young himself. But his very age—he is in his early fif-ties—is a challenge to the vigor and tireless drive and enthusiasm that belong to youth.

Back from World War I, where he had seen action with Colonel Patton's tanks on the Belgian border, Conrad Schatte found for himself a wife and a job selling trucks. Both the wife and the job were wholly satisfactory, but what Con really yearned for was a business of his own.

But soon children were coming along and Con hesitated to take the risk. However, he saved his money and eventually made the break and set up a little auto mobile repair shop. Unhappily the field was so crowded and competition so keen that after a few years Con called it quits and took a job with an oil company.

Then one day, shortly before Pearl Harbor, a friend gave Con a Great Dane puppy, Rhett Butler III, and that changed the whole course of his life. An inseparable companion to his wife and youngsters, the huge pup went along on their auto excursions, all of which added up to too big a load for the little family car. The purchase of a secondhand station wagon was the answer to the dilemma.

Along about this time, in 1942, Con volunteered for his second world war. In 1945, back in this country after being partly disabled in a bomber crash, he determined to have an enterprise of his own: he did not want to burden another man's business with his disability. But first he must see to his indispensable station wagon; its woodwork eaten with dry rot, it was sadly in need of repair. To his astonishment, he had to comb Detroit, the "Motor City," before he could find a repairman, an oldtime carriage maker, who knew how to do the work.

That gave Con his idea for a business in an uncrowded field. When in southern California to take final leave of the Army, he was amazed at the thousands of station wagons he saw. Here, he reasoned, was a chance for a *different* business—a shop specializing exclusively in the supercare and repair of station wagons. Woodworking had always been a hobby of his, anyway. Action followed idea—and Con moved his family and station wagon and Great Dane to Los Angeles.

Today, on Hollywood's famed Vine Street, one of the sights to see is Station Wagon Rejuvenation, a "beauty" shop from which emerge daily once-haggard old wagons shining with a blooming schoolgirl complexion.

Station wagons of all ages and stages of disrepair come in for a beauty treatment. Hesitant owners of ancient wagons will park at the curb and ask timidly if it is too late for anything to be done for the old girl. Always such relics stay for rejuvenation because Con knows how to work miracles in bringing them back to life. When his first customer came into the shop to pick up his station wagon, the man flatly refused to believe that the new and shining beauty was his. Finally convinced that it was, he rapturously kissed Con on both cheeks.

Sportsmen come in for specially designed gun cabinets, refrigeration, cooking, and sleeping installations—conveniences that add to their enjoyment of their wagons—all done with superb craftsmanship.

The gun cabinets are only one of Con's special jobs. For a mother it was a bed for her baby; for a movie dog trainer it was a fancy dog pen; for one of the studios it was a tricky portable telephone cabinet. For a florist a special rack for flowers was constructed, and for a dry cleaner Con installed an ingenious hanging arrangement for clothes. He gets a lot of orders for the installation of camping equipment—beds, stoves, and refrigerators. He stands ready to meet any request, no matter how novel and startling it may be.

Conrad Schatte's unique business is a success—a big success that is growing steadily and making it necessary right along to add additional craftsmen to his staff. Con thinks that veterans in other parts of the country ought to copy his idea. To them he has this to say:

"The care and repair of station wagons will pay a good income even if one does no more than clean and refinish the wooden bodies. To render a complete service a cabinetmaker's skill is needed; this can be the proprietor's or it can be found and hired. An oldtime cabinetmaker is the man to look for. In time he can be an expert on station wagon cabinetry. Knowledge of woods, wood finishing, and the tools of the trade, such as drill presses, table saw, handsaw, drills, grinders, clamps, and by all means fine cabinetmaker's tools are a must. There must be readily available a supply of seasoned maple, birch, oak, and the ornamental veneers that make up the panels. All of this may seem like a lot, but actually around four hundred to five hundred dollars is sufficient capital for enough equipment and supplies to get started with. Added tools and materials can be bought as the business progresses."

Con makes it clear that the beginner will not find his business a gold mine the first year. "What new business is?" he asks. "It is my observation," he says, "that most new enterprises are darn lucky to break even the first year or two. I think the young fellow who starts up a business like mine can safely figure he will net around two thousand dollars, on a one-man operation, during his first twelve months. After that the gross take can run quite high: the net depends, as in any business, on careful, economical management and hustle."

Con recommends a main thoroughfare location where motor traffic is heavy. He also advises some moderate advertising, and has found mimeographed letters, small ads, in newspapers, and a sizable ad in the classified telephone directory to be resultful. "But my best advertising," he says, "has been the high quality of my work."

Con Schatte is a station wagon enthusiast. Listen to him: "No longer is the station wagon a mere conveyance for guests and their luggage, or something to run back and forth from the beach. Today it represents a way of life. It is the movie star's indispensable: it is the car for the full rich life; with one or two seats removed, it handles loads like a truck; or with seats enough for a crowd, it is either a bus or a limousine. Babies and small toddlers are happy and safe on even long rides in their own compartment where they can play or sleep as suits their fancy. With their fine good looks, today's wagons may be likened to the carriages of yesteryear—at home on the finest of boulevards or the roughest of roads—and that is where you see them more and more every day. Truly adaptable, truly convertible, they are perfectly suited to the individual's purpose."

A fair-sized city or marketing area, preferably in a recreational area or one abounding in ranches, farms, or country places, will furnish the trade needed. One man can run such a shop and do all the work himself, but Con promises that more than one man will be needed because the business is sure to grow. His did.

HE UPHOLSTERS OLD PIANOS

Before the war Charles C. Nields, of Los Angeles, a Navy veteran, had worked at interior decorating. One of his big headaches had been the old-fashioned, bulky, outmoded piano. Such eyesores had spoiled many a room where he had been called in to do a bit of decorating.

Often the owners had refused to part with their instruments, either for sentimental reasons or because their budgets would not permit a new one. Sometimes they protested that their mellow old pianos had incomparable tone.

Back from the war, this thought occurred to Nields: "Why not upholster the piano and treat it as a handsome piece of furniture and not as a huge wooden box?" He began to experiment with techniques, and what he developed was so novel that in 1946 a United States design patent was issued to him; and in addition a "means and method" patent is now pending.

The Nields idea cuts down and streamlines the old crates to an absolute minimum in size, lopping off rococo molding, carvings, and gewgaws, and replacing the ornate legs with ones of simple design. The front is trimmed down at the top in a graceful tapering design. The entire cabinet, after first being padded with cotton, is covered with damask, mohair, plastic, leatherette, etc., in almost inexhaustible combinations of color, designs, and effects, the whole in keeping with what Nields calls "the theme of the room furnishings." Trimming nails and tufting add to the interest of his effects.

The Nields idea, which is entirely original in the piano field, is a huge success. He feels that it offers a fine business opportunity to any man anywhere who has a knack with tools and an eye for beauty. Under his patents he is permitted to franchise and license his methods, and he believes that the "upholstered piano" will soon be seen in homes all over the nation.

OPERATION JANITOR

Consider now the case of Alex Paul Peet and Harry Roy Touchy, two Texas boys who were star footballers at Baylor University before playing stellar roles in the Pacific—Paul as an infantryman for twenty-nine months, Roy as a lieutenant in the Navy for a year and a half.

The war over, the boys were eager to have a fling at some sort of enterprise of their own in Houston. They liked people and made friends easily, and they felt that in selling they might find their opportunity. So they set up a little sales agency and, joining their

middle names, called it Paul Roy and Company. Their line consisted of a wide variety of cleaning supplies—washing powders,
disinfectants, solvents, waxes, brushes, brooms, mops, etc.

But they soon found to their dismay that it was no go. Well-
entrenched competition was not yielding an inch. Prospective buyers were friendly enough, but the supplies offered by Paul and Roy
had no special virtues as against competitive products.

"We don't need your supplies," building managers told them,
"but we are sure short of manpower to use the supplies we have
now."

At this point their infant company only a few weeks old, the
two young veterans were just about convinced they had better get
busy and find jobs. Running an enterprise of their own was tougher
than they thought. Then one happy day, mulling over their problem, they hit on their big idea—Operation Janitor—a cleaning business on a streamlined mass production basis. So the building managers are desperately short of manpower. Okay, let's give it to them.

Their manpower problem they solved at one stroke by putting
their idea up to the Veterans' Placement Bureau. "Sure," said the
bureau, "there are a lot of young huskies here at the University of
Houston, all war veterans, who are eager to get part-time work.
We'll help you line them up."

But the rest of it wasn't that easy. Paul and Roy had only four
thousand dollars between them, and their cleaning equipment—
electric floor-cleaning machines, ladders, brushes, etc.—ate up
three thousand dollars of that. And the building managers failed
to put out the welcome mat as quickly as had been anticipated.
The idea of a bunch of college kids shining up their buildings was
a little too startling for them—which is understandable, Paul explains, because expert "janitoring" involves many technical problems.

What business they got at the start came through door-to-door
canvassing, but it was dishearteningly slow work. Soon their remaining thousand dollars of capital was gone, and for nine months
neither Paul nor Roy drew a cent of pay or profit.

But at last came the break they had been hoping for—a contract to do a cellar-to-roof cleaning job on the big Medical Arts

Building. Here was a chance to show the skeptics what the college kids could do. Sixty of the boys, working from 5 P.M. to midnight, washing, scrubbing, waxing, polishing, did that stint in a week. Paul and Roy, hanging precariously out of windows and teetering on ladders, were right in there pitching with the boys. Then, the very next week, the vets hung up some kind of world's record giving the works to the elegant thousand-room Rice Hotel. Those two jobs broke the ice and were given fine publicity in the Houston newspapers. Profitable new contracts are now pouring in every week without let-up, and nearly two hundred veteran-students are on the part-time pay roll of the company at a dollar per hour.

"Our success is due in part," says Paul, "to the wonderful morale of the boys. They are fast and well-disciplined, but they contrive to have fun along with their efficiency. For instance, posing heroically on twenty-five-foot ladders in the lobby of the Rice Hotel, they gloried in the admiration of pretty girls, both employees and guests. But what has counted most," continues Paul, "is the fact that we are meeting a neglected need in an uncrowded field."

Paul and Roy also give credit to improved cleaning techniques. They are quick to try out the newest notions in the janitoring business, and many improvements are the ideas of themselves and their boys. One innovation is a liquid detergent called Alcodine, a formula worked out by one of Paul's buddies in the war. Alcodine is a noncorrosive, nonalkali, noncaustic chemical that saves hours of elbow work. It performs miracles in bringing dirt to the surface where it can he wiped away with a flick of the wrist. Paul and Roy, in collaboration with the inventor, plan to market Alcodine nationally.

Paul Roy and Company has no hard-and-fast method of charging for its work. "What and how we charge," says Paul, "depends upon the job. Large buildings are usually charged a flat rate, whereas small places and private homes are ordinarily charged by the hour. Occasionally on special jobs we work on a cost-plus basis. We find that we must figure our bids very carefully, a lesson we learned the hard way when occasionally we bid too low. There is much more to this business than meets the eye."

Although Paul and Roy are now making plans to expand their business by establishing "Operation Janitor" in a few other cities, they seek no monopoly. They believe their idea and general plan for operation can be just as successful for other veterans in other cities all over the country. They recommend not less than three thousand dollars' worth of equipment, and they believe that no profits should be expected from the business for at least six months. "I am sure we have a swell idea," Paul says, "but few ideas are good enough to build a profitable business overnight." He urges that a few hundred dollars should be invested in advertising at the outset, and he recommends letters as an effective low-cost medium.

SWAG IN SWAPPING TIES

In Wilmington, Delaware, are two young brothers—ex-officers of the Navy, Jake and Bernie Kreshtool—who are making originality pay off handsomely. Their curious little business is the only one of its kind in the world.

Out of the Navy after five years of service (Jake had been a lieutenant commander and Bernie a lieutenant), the boys wanted to work for themselves. Jake, an advertising copywriter before the war, opened up a small advertising office in Wilmington. Bernie, aiming to finish his studies and set himself up as a dentist, came up with the big idea.

Before the war, during Christmas vacation from college, Bernie had clerked in a Wilmington haberdashery. Sadly he had watched women select neckties he was sure would never be worn by their conservative husbands or boy friends, men he knew as customers.

Out of this observation came Tieswap, a sort of central mail-order exchange permitting men to swap ties with one another. Starting less than a year ago, and working only three spare-time evenings a week, the firm is now netting around four hundred fifty dollars a month extra over regular earnings. Through little classified ads in national magazines they arrange necktie swaps with people all over the United States. Their advertising cost is a fraction over six cents per swap—an amazingly low figure.

Their ingenious scheme seems to have potent lure. Here is the way it works. Henry Jones, of Portland, Oregon, has six ties in good condition, but he is tired of them or never did like them. William

Smith, of Portland, Maine, has four still-good ties that have lost their charm for him, plus those two Aunt Sarah gave him on his birthday. Jones sends his ties to Tieswap, and so does Smith. Any number is acceptable, even one; the average number sent is five.

Tieswap, which has a favorable contract with the best dry cleaner in town, brightens up the ties like new, engineers the swap, and collects a fee of a dollar for the service. If Jones has written in that he is partial to emerald green ties, he doesn't get Smith's, which are brown; he gets Murphy's. If, like their undertaker client in Utah, he wants black, he gets Navy ties, of which the boys have an abundance. The aim is to please. The boys sent bright red ties to a man living in Moscow, Idaho. Writing that it wasn't funny, the Soviet-hater returned them indignantly. The ties he had originally sent in, bearing the Moscow label, went to a woman in Connecticut, who told her husband the gift was something she had picked up at Lake Success. Everybody is happy all around.

Believe it or not, these two young vets in ten months have swapped 23,580 neckties for 4,718 customers. "The business is growing every week," reports Jake, "and now that Bernie is back at Temple, it's going to keep me jumping." Where the idea will lead to eventually Jake does not know. Ties from foreign countries—Canada, Venezuela, Cuba, the Bahamas—are beginning to trickle in, and it could be that Tieswap may soon be an international enterprise.

What's more, the carriage trade likes the idea. New clients currently include two United States senators, a famous New York cartoonist, a wealthy Washington publisher, a vice-admiral, and a few well-known industrialists (including a duPont). An experienced mail-order man declares he sees no reason why the young business should not grow, even with only left-handed attention, to ten times its present size.

Sustenance for Starving Students

Then there's Elmo Geppelt, a twenty-four-year-old 8th Air Force veteran who is an electrical engineering student at the University of Kansas at Lawrence. Elmo with a wife and a fifteen-month-old son soon found his GI school allowance, ninety dollars, wasn't enough. Elmo's idea came to him via a hungry stomach. During all-night sessions with his textbooks, his wife would sustain him with hot sandwiches and coffee. "I have a notion, Betty," he said to her on one of these occasions, "that hundreds of night-owl students would like to have a delicious snack like this delivered to their rooms."

That notion began Geeps Food Service for studious night-oil burners. Every day except Fridays and Saturdays, five automobiles, owned and operated by students, make nightly deliveries to fifty fraternity and sorority houses; and the delivery is made, if requested, right to the bedside of the student. The hot dishes are kept warm in insulated heated boxes; the soft drinks are kept cold in special ice-packed containers.

Betty, who runs the kitchen and its six cooks, is a graduate of the university; hence she knows what kind of snacks the student savors most. Elmo, who while in high school was a cook for Boy Scout summer camps, helps out.

Elmo's business is grossing over $1,500 a month. He estimates that if he could devote full time to it he could easily net three hundred dollars to five hundred dollars a month. No less than eighteen students are being helped through school by his enterprise: the six cooks are students' wives, and each of the six cars is manned by two student veterans.

Walter Slovenski, GI student and varsity footballer at Syracuse, operates a somewhat similar enterprise. Having converted an old car into a small restaurant on wheels (which he calls "Whimpy"), he hawks his viands every day on the campus driveways to the always-hungry students. Walter does so well that he is able to contribute to the support of his parents.

CAMPUS CANDY CAPITALISTS

Three juniors in the School of Commerce at Northwestern, Joseph M. Decker, Donald C. Loose, and Frank C. Nicholas, who had been airplane pilots during the war, are now operating a campus business that is said to be the only student enterprise of its kind in the country.

Their Northwestern-U-Select-It Company vends candy in coin-operated machines placed, under an exclusive contract arrangement, in every sorority and fraternity house on the campus, and in banks, business offices, and factories around Evanston. A student majoring in accounting keeps their books, and three other students help them service their machines, all of them working on a profit-sharing basis.

Their business is running smoothly and paying satisfactory profits, but at the start the boys had to use all the resourcefulness they had. The school's administrative officers were doubtful about the desirability of the idea, and only after a lot of persuasion did the boys get the green light. The clincher was an offer to contribute five per cent of the profits to the Student Governing Board. Manufacturers, hard put to supply their old accounts with candy, extended no glad hand to these campus greenhorns. Their candy, warehoused in Frank's room at the Beta Theta Pi house, taught them a hard lesson about every candyman's dilemma—melted chocolate. Nonfunctioning machines, tampered with by prankster students, was another headache.

The boys' biggest problem is that of keeping to a work schedule that permits neither studies nor business to be cheated. None of the three had any college training prior to the war, and they must soak up as much education as they can in the four years allowed by the GI bill. Happily, their little business is prospering, and it promises to finance them through law school later. The boys feel that enterprises similar to theirs would do well on many campuses.

Dollars in Downing Dust

Read now what imagination and hustle did for Robert McQuade and Anthony Dincalci, students at the University of Arizona. Bob has a three-year record on Guam as an Army Air Force pilot. Tony has nearly five years behind him in the Navy.

Both boys are married and one of them, Tony, is the father of a two-year-old son. Although they were housed cheaply in Quonset huts, they found ninety dollars a month wasn't enough. They earned some money around their Quonset campus by doing gardening and they sold ads in the school paper, but still couldn't make ends meet. What the boys hankered for was a dependable little business of some kind they could run in their spare time.

Out of their observation of two facts—that sandy dust on Tucson's outlying streets and roads was a dreadful nuisance; that hundreds of gallons of used oil, drained out of crank cases every day, were being thrown away—emerged an idea.

The two students owned a beat-up 1932 Packard sedan which they stripped and converted into a pick-up. Then they mounted three 5-gallon tanks on the rear and installed a two-horsepower motor with a pump to force out the oil through ordinary lawn, sprinklers. Their actual cash outlay was three hundred dollars. Putting the contraption together was a cinch: Tony had been a plumber, a machinist, and a stationary engineer in the Navy.

Overnight they had a business. Their tanks filled with 150 gallons of waste oil supplied free by service stations, they set out for the dusty roads on the outskirts of the city. Soliciting door to door, they passed out cards displaying their slogan: "We serve the supper crust, we oil your roads and lay your dust." Whole blocks gave them joyful welcome. What this enterprise yields in profits the boys have ruled a state secret. "But we can tell you we do well," they assert, "and when we graduate we expect to have a nest egg in the bank." Their idea, they think, ought to do well in thousands of dusty communities.

Their Jalopies Pay Off

For George Demmon and Richard Lyon, students at Cornell, it was a case of quitting school or adding to their GI allowances. Both veterans are married, George the father of one child, Dick of two, and they quickly discovered that occasional spare-time jobs at sixty-five cents an hour (the average student rate of pay in Ithaca) left them short.

At Cornell the veterans' housing projects are situated so far from the retail district that they get little or no delivery service from Ithaca stores. That gave the boys their idea. Each had a car of ancient vintage, and for one of these jalopies they built a trailer. They then talked with local egg producers and bakeries and offered to deliver fresh eggs and bakery goods daily to the homes in the GI housing project area. It was a good deal—until local stores, feeling the competition, put the heat on the suppliers (a mean move that back-fired when the lads went to nearby Syracuse for their wares).

Working about twenty hours a week, on a commission basis, they serve 300 student families; in addition, they supply a newly formed Veterans' Cooperative food store. With their GI allotment both George and Dick have incomes of around two hundred dollars a month.

BOOKKEEPING ON WHEELS

An old idea, but one still new in most parts of the Country, is the "Cunocar Accounting Service," an idea conceived by Cuno R. Bryant of Portland, Oregon. There's a good chance you won't find anything comparable in your community. In all metropolitan cities there are many congested business neighborhoods offering a fine opportunity for such a service.

Simply described, Cunocar is an accounting service on wheels. An office built on a truck body, it is equipped with a desk, a bookkeeping machine, a typewriter, a filing cabinet—in fact, with about every business tool except a telephone. It brings expert bookkeeping to the door of the small businessman—grocer, druggist, baker, hardwareman, garageman—whose requirements justify neither costly machines nor a full-time bookkeeper. The customer's books are brought out to the Cunocar and put into up-to-the-minute shape. The Cunocar calls at intervals agreed on—once every day or week or month—according to the clients' needs.

Cuno Bryant, his capital only four hundred dollars of borrowed money, built his first mobile office on an old Ford truck, in 1922. Cunocars are now operating in a dozen or more cities. About forty veterans are now establishing Cunocar service in various parts of the country. But the field is still virgin. Bookkeeping on wheels is still a new kind of business that fills a need long ignored.

The Old Music Box Comes Back

About thirteen years ago, Lloyd G. Kelley, a traveling salesman for a food company, one boresome evening wandered into an ancient secondhand store on one of Boston's crooked side streets.

Because he did that Lloyd is no longer peddling groceries. He is the owner of a revived enterprise that was supposedly as dead as grandma's spinning wheel. Hardheaded businessmen laughed at Lloyd when he talked over his idea with them. So for ten years after his fateful visit that day to the old secondhand store he played with his notion as a hobby.

For many years Lloyd had been hankering for a small business of his own, but he was hesitant. He wanted to go into an enterprise that was different. He couldn't see much future in another "me too" undertaking—a gas station, a restaurant, a fix-it shop, or a haberdashery. Besides, he hadn't been able to save much on his earnings as a salesman, and most of his ideas called for too much capital.

Three years ago he quit his job and made his hobby his business. He is glad he did. "My enterprise may never make me a millionaire," he says, "but still it is the best thing that ever happened to me. Of greater importance, I love my work—and I have never been so happy in my life."

What's more, thousands of American families are happy about the whole thing too.

What Lloyd saw in that dark and dusty antique shop that day was an antiquated music box. Made of walnut, superbly hand-carved, it was a beautiful specimen of early American woodwork. Strangely enough, it was the first music box he had ever seen, and he was fascinated. An old disk tinkled out "Home, Sweet Home," and Lloyd, mellow with sentiment, almost bought the machine. The deal fell through when the shopkeeper told him that this disk comprised his entire stock of musical selections

A week or two later Lloyd ran across two other music boxes— one an old Regina type, the other a Swiss model—in a secondhand store in Chelsea, Massachusetts. This time he capitulated—although the mechanism was out of joint and wouldn't work. He had to hunt for three weeks all over Boston to find an oldtime clock-

maker who knew how to make repairs. He managed also after dili-
gent search to track down a half dozen disks of mid-Victorian song
hits.

Then he gave a "musicale" for a few of his friends. Several of
his nostalgic guests, raving over the sweet melodies of grand-
mother's day, asked Lloyd to find a nice old music box for them.
Haunting antique and secondhand shops all over New England,
Lloyd managed to uncover a considerable number of rare pieces.
In the meantime his friends were spreading his fame and orders
for the boxes were coming from all over.

But despite this growing interest Lloyd continued to sell groceries, and his music boxes, although they made a little money for
him, were strictly a spare-time hobby. Bankers and businessmen
had little faith in the idea that disk music could stage a comeback.
And he was confronted by a serious obstacle in the terrific shortage of records: plenty of families all over the country had music
boxes, many of them treasured heirlooms, stored in their attics,
but their disks had long since disappeared.

Music-box owners, hearing of Lloyd's hobby, besieged him to
find disks for them. This inspired his big idea. He saw fine business possibilities, not in collecting and selling old music boxes (except as an incidental activity), but in making disks to supply what
obviously was a sizable pent-up demand.

He was all set to quit his job and go to it until he discovered
that he would need a small fortune to set up a factory for making
disks. Assuming that craftsmen skilled in such work could be found,
which was improbable, a lot of special equipment and machinery
would have to be made.

It all looked pretty hopeless until Lloyd put his problem to Mr.
Maurice Chaillet of Rahway, New Jersey. Mr. Chaillet was the
owner of the master plates and machinery of the old Regina music-box outfit, a company more or less inactive since the turn of
the century, when its death knell had been sounded by the introduction of the phonograph. Mr. Chaillet, just as tenderly sentimental as Lloyd over the sweet old music-box melodies, fell in readily
with the idea. He agreed to sell the Regina machinery and plates
to Lloyd for a small sum and accept payment in small installments.

On that happy day, nearly three years ago, Lloyd's ten-year hobby became his business: he set up shop in Hanover, Massachusetts. During his first year his production was confined to disks made with the old master plates bought from Mr. Chaillet. These disks, fifteen and one-half inches in diameter, can be played only on the Regina disk-type music box. Lloyd plans later to produce other types of records.

During the last two years he has been enlarging his repertoire, his specialty being Christmas music, in response to a flood of popular demand. Just prior to the holidays last year, Lloyd and his two assistants worked day and night trying to keep up with orders for "Noel," "White Christmas," "Jingle Bells," and "Hark! the Herald Angels Sing."

Orders come from every state in the Union and even from Canada, Australia, England, and the Continent. Many well-known statesmen, corporation presidents, musicians, writers, and painters are among Lloyd's Clientele. His files are bulging with letters from customers telling him that their music boxes and disks are among their most prized possessions.

One charming old lady had her chauffeur drive her all the way from New York to Hanover— "just to express my appreciation in person to you." (She was eighty at the time.)

Lloyd, a gentle, serene man of about fifty, said to me, with a contented smile, "I have been feeling pretty good about that visit of hers ever since. Boogie-woogie hasn't got a monopoly yet."

DENVER'S NOVEL PARKING SERVICE

Marvin Goldfarb, back from the war and looking for a way to earn a living in Denver, was annoyed every time he tried to park his car in the downtown business and shopping area. "I couldn't buy a handkerchief," he says, "without walking four to six blocks from the place I parked my car."

That gave him an idea, and he put it up to his buddy, another veteran, Marvin Pooley. The idea: a big parking lot outside the congested area, and a station wagon shuttle service for shoppers between the lot and the downtown stores. The hitch was that between them the two Marvins had very little money.

Seeking financial help, they talked up their idea to veterans' bureaus, the city administration, the Chamber of Commerce, the banks, and the department stores. Everybody said it was a swell idea and let's do it, but the net result in cash help was so small that the two veterans had to scurry around in search of additional assistance.

At this bleak point one of Denver's biggest department stores, the May Company, offered them immediate cash help and an exclusive contract arrangement to shuttle its customers. Further help was offered them when a Denver automobile agency, listening to their problem with a sympathetic ear, provided them with eight new Ford station wagons on extremely easy payment terms. That was less than two years ago. Today, out of the red, the business is solidly established and its popularity is spreading fast.

Here's the way the business works: the shopper drives her car into the lot, parks it, gets into a station wagon, and is taken to the May Store. After she has done her shopping, she returns in a later station wagon to the lot, bringing with her a validated sales slip, which, no matter how small her purchase, entitles her to a free hour of parking (ten cents per hour thereafter). She gets into her car and goes home. No bother, no worry, and no waiting—the station wagons make a trip every three minutes.

Anybody (May customer or not) can hop aboard a station wagon. There is no charge for the ride, since charging would infringe on the tramway company's franchise. Parking charges account for only part of the income; oil, gas, and car washings add substantially to profits.

Edison once said that when something irritates you, don't grumble—do something about it. That's the way to get ideas. Marvin Goldfarb, irritated by parking conditions in Denver, invented for himself and his buddy a fine new business. Such an enterprise could be equally successful in cities all over America.

CHILDREN'S OUTGROWN CLOTHING STORE

Don't let it be thought that men have a corner on imagination and initiative. There's Mrs. Alberta Drake, of Denver, for instance.

About a year ago she was a saleslady in the boys' department of a Denver department store. Every day she listened to customers, many of them well-off, complain that their closets were full of children's clothing that was outgrown but not outworn. These parents had paid such prices for the garments that they disliked giving them away. Then there were other customers who wanted clothes of a quality they couldn't afford, today's prices being what they are.

Pondering this, Mrs. Drake had an idea. She and her husband had recently bought a home which included a small store building in front. Half of this building was Mr. Drake's workshop; the other half was used for storage. Why not convert this storage half into a store dealing exclusively in children's outgrown clothing?

Action followed the idea. Mrs. Drake had a small savings account, and with a little of this money she bought a few fixtures and some drapes and cases. At the outset, she didn't quit the department store. "I wanted to be real sure of myself," she explains, "before I gave up my job downtown." So for nine months she tended her shop in the evenings, while a temporary saleswoman took care of customers in the daytime. In that short time the business grew so rapidly that, three months ago, she resigned her job and now runs her store alone.

Mrs. Drake buys no merchandise outright for her Children's Outgrown Clothing Store. All clothing is taken in on consignment. When Mrs. Jones brings in an armful of clothing she and Mrs. Drake get together and agree on the price for each garment. To these prices Mrs. Drake adds a reasonable mark-up for herself. She agrees to keep the clothing for two months; if it is not sold by then, the owner may have it back or leave it. "Nearly everyone leaves it," says Mrs. Drake.

Most of her customers are the persons who bring in outgrown clothing to sell. Almost invariably they see a garment or two their children can use, and they buy it. Her advertising expense has been very small. The Denver newspapers have considered her project unique and newsworthy and have given her generous publicity. But her best advertising has been word-of-mouth boosting of her business by satisfied customers.

Streamlined Baby Sitting

Then there is the successful experience of Miss Geneva Corlett. Her enterprise wasn't exactly new; but in Toledo, her home town, it was new; not just another "me too" idea.

It is almost a certainty that your luck has been better than Geneva's. When she was eleven days old a tumor was removed from her spine, and she has been confined to a wheel chair ever since. Yet this handicap has not stopped her from building up the profitable business she runs from that chair in her home.

She offers something Toledo wanted but didn't get until she set up shop—a streamlined, smoothly operating, highly systematized service she calls "Baby Sitters United." While there are somewhat similar services in a few other cities, Miss Corlett at this time of writing has no organized competition in Toledo. She is most modest about her success. "I'm sure I'm not talented in any way," she says. "I began by simply asking parents what they expected of a baby sitter, and what they expect is what I do my best to give them."

Miss Corlett has set up definite hard-and-fast standards. Her sitters must be at least of high-school age, and they must come recommended by a minister or a physician. They are allowed only such freedom as parents specifically give them. They are not allowed to entertain friends; they must not play the radio or the phonograph without permission; and long telephone chit-chats are strictly taboo. Girls with little experience are not sent out on difficult cases; to parents who think baby needs special care, Miss Corlett will send, upon request, a sitter who is a retired trained or practical nurse.

She has a code for parents, too. The sitter must be asked to do no chores except those having to do with the needs of the children they are watching. It is mandatory for parents to keep the sitter advised at all times of their whereabouts. At any hour after 9 P.M., it is up to the parents to see that the sitter is escorted safely home.

Miss Corlett's office is simplicity itself. It consists of a desk, a telephone, and a small file containing two sets of cards. On one set are the names of approximately one hundred girls and women who have qualified as Corlett baby sitters. In addition to phone numbers and addresses, other pertinent data are noted on these cards—

the age and experience of the sitter, on what days and hours she is usually available, etc. On the other set are recorded the names of her regular clients, about a hundred in all, and certain pertinent data about them. Included among her clients, incidentally, are a number of women's organizations—they have found that Baby Sitters United is just what they need to get bigger turnouts at their club luncheons.

Miss Corlett's advertising expense has been practically nothing. Her enterprise is sponsored by Toledo's Crippled Children's Society; and this organization, aided and abetted by women's clubs and the Rotary Club, has seen to it that the Corlett project has had abundant newspaper publicity. The girls' dean at the high school keeps Miss Corlett supplied with sitters.

The parents and not the sitter pay Miss Corlett's fee, thirty-five cents for each call, two dollars for six calls, or five dollars for eighteen. The sitter herself is paid forty cents an hour until midnight, seventy cents an hour after that. These charges are no higher—and very often are lower—than is customarily paid in Toledo for free-lance, nonregistered sitters.

Madison Doll Hospital

Not original, either, is the idea of a doll hospital. But Madison, Wisconsin, didn't have one—and the need seemingly went unnoticed by everybody except Mrs. Eva M. Sullivan.

She collected dolls, purely as a hobby, for ten or twelve years, and in 1946 decided that something ought to be done about the total lack of "surgical" service for Madison's doll population. So she set up the Madison Doll Hospital, a business-for-profit enterprise owned and operated solely by herself.

At her hospital missing limbs are replaced, fractured skulls are mended, and battered bodies are made whole again. For some dolls entirely new bodies are provided. For others new eyes or new wigs are needed; for those which have lost their voices Mrs. Sullivan has a wide variety of "larynxes" on hand. If the doll's hair lacks luster, it is given an expert beauty treatment.

To date some seven hundred "patients" have gone through the Madison Doll Hospital.

Riches in Rocks

Here is a story about a man whose name is S. N. Green, and who is now living in the tiny mountain village of Bayfield, in Colorado. About seven years ago, Mr. Green, bordering on sixty and thinking of his impending retirement from his United States Government job in Chicago, took a stroll one Sunday along the beach on Chicago's lake front.

As he sauntered along in the sand, his head down as he pondered his problem, he noticed and picked up a little stone of unusual shape and coloring. He took it home and tried to polish it. His poor success challenged his interest, and soon the collecting and polishing of stones became his hobby.

Then Mr. Green had an idea. He would collect, cut, polish, and sell his stones to other amateur collectors, all over the world. In his leisure time, pending his retirement, he worked at his new hobby. But Chicago was no place for a collector of stones; he must go and live and work among them. So urgent was his impulse that Mr. Green moved himself to Bayfield, in the heart of the Colorado Rockies.

Mr. Green's home, which is also his workshop, is a little white house against a lovely mountain backdrop. From here he maintains contact with five thousand stone collectors and lapidarists everywhere. His sales exceed ten thousand dollars a year. Now sixty-six years old, he has the energy and enthusiasm of a healthy man of fifty, and it is inspiring to watch his eyes light up as he talks about his hobby.

"But my biggest dividend isn't the money I make," Mr. Green explains. "I love my work. One idea leads to another and my days are full of interest. I think I am the most contented man in the world. It is shocking that of those who retire most are killed off by discontent and idleness in four to five years."

Business Born in a Backyard

There is inspiration, too, in the story of Paul Pueschel, of Glencoe, Illinois. About eight years ago, Mr. Pueschel, also nearing retirement age, had an idea that has not only given him a comfortable income but health and contentment.

For years he had loved to watch wild birds in his garden, and it was his habit to feed them. But he had never been able to find a feeding station that would be a sure-fire attraction to birds, keep the birds in full view while feeding or perching, stoutly resist strong winds, and be proof against such raiders as cats, squirrels, rats, and chipmunks.

"Giving the matter some thought," says Mr. Pueschel, "I had an idea. Why not invent such a feeding station myself? I got into action immediately. Then and there ended my fruitless and often discontented loafing around the house. I went to work with a burst of energy such as I hadn't known in a long time. After a number of unsuccessful attempts I had what I sought—a bird-feeding station I call The Squirrel's Defeat."

That was eight years ago. Today, Mr. Pueschel's thriving little company, which he calls Audubon Workshop, cannot take care of the constantly growing demand for its product. "Although I am well up in years," says Mr. Pueschel, "I have never been busier in my life. And I am enjoying myself immensely."

LUCKY CLOVER FARMER

For sheer novelty consider the enterprise of Archer F. Herrick of Saco, Maine, veteran of World War I. Archer is a multiple-leaf clover farmer catering to thousands of people who are eager to improve their luck. His wares include not only the popular four-leaf clover, but specimens with five, six, seven, eight, and nine leaves. Number Seven, as one would expect, is most in demand by the superstitious. Archer, who boasts that he is the only man in the world who has propagated a nine-leaf clover, promises that ultimately he expects to include a twelve-leafer in his line.

Archer, who came out of the first war a semi-invalid, helped all he could in World War II working in the navy yard at Portsmouth, New Hampshire. In his spare time he made an even greater contribution by mailing multi-leaf clovers free to hundreds of GIs who requested them. In answer to one request Archer asked the commanding officer of the unit if all the boys wanted lucky clovers. The answer was an enthusiastic "yes" and Archer sent, in one big parcel-post bundle, enough for everybody. After that, stamps for his shipments to the GIs nearly broke him.

Archer's business began as a hobby. For his health's sake he had to spend a lot of time in his little garden. Often he was despondent, and one day when he was feeling very low he searched in his garden for a four-leaf clover "just for luck." Then and there began his career as a multiple-leaf farmer, a career that met his doctor's specifications by keeping him out of doors on every fair day.

Beginning from scratch, Archer made himself all authority on clovers. Developing an original process of root culture, he succeeded after two years of experiment in propagating his many-leafed varieties from four-leaf clover seed.

Archer's clover farm, his hobby, yielded enough to pay for his home. A little story about him in *Profitable Hobbies* brought him a flood of letters, and how his expanding business is taking all of his time. As an additional source of revenue he is now selling pedigreed clover house plants, which are amazingly large and beautiful, as well as his lucky leaves.

In his novel clover farm Archer Herrick has not only a profitable business, but an occupation that pays extra dividends in health and contentment.

18

Imagination and Information—The Unbeatable Team

We have told you in this book about what we consider to be the chief ingredient to anyone's success, and we have illustrated every phase of the use of imagination by specific examples of men and women who, with no more ability than those around them, achieved mightily because they had the use of this power at their disposal.

Perhaps you may have the idea by now that using imagination is enough to assure your success in any venture you undertake. And it is—provided you link up imagination with information to make the unbeatable team.

Unfortunately, there have been many men and women who have used the most brilliant imaginations possible, but have failed because they have not added information to their formula. It takes both. It takes imagination, as we have shown you throughout this book, to give life, verve, force, to a project. It takes information to make sure that this life, verve, force, will be directed where it will do the most good.

You see, imagination is like any powerful force in that it can be used improperly so that its vast powers do harm. Dynamite is a useful explosive which, when properly directed, works miracles of force; ignorantly, improperly used, it has blown many of its users to bits. Electric energy is undeniably a powerful factor in serving man, yet thousands of persons have been electrocuted because they used it improperly. It is the same with imagination.

One of the most brilliant users of imagination we ever knew was forever conceiving ideas which anyone could see were miracles of imagination. He was an inventor. He died in poverty. The reason for that was his unwillingness to link facts with his ideas, to mix information with his imagination and stir well before using. To illustrate: he at one time spent several years perfecting an invention he was sure would serve mankind. Reading of a disastrous flood which had washed away a railroad bridge and caused a long train to plunge into a river, drowning over fifty persons, this kind-hearted inventor decided he would put a stop to such violent deaths. He invented life rafts to be carried on every train. Whenever a car went into a river all the passengers had to do to save themselves was to board the rafts. It took imagination to conceive such an idea. But there was no information invoked. The inventor disregarded the fact that so few railroad passengers are drowned that it is a negligible factor. He could have saved himself hours and hours of work and scores of heartbreaks if he had inquired before he acted.

The archives of the United States Patent Office are filled with equally grotesque ideas, and the life stories of millions of men and women contain tragedies of persons who put their money, their time, their energy, upon projects that were doomed to failure because they lacked the backing of information.

All such catastrophes could be avoided by making information a partner in any thinking undertaking and seeking a background of facts.

In his stimulating book *What's Holding You Back?* Allan B. Chalfont suggests a three-point procedure as the imperative first step in tackling any undertaking. It is this:

    1. Get command of specific *facts* about the subject.
    2. Get command of *more facts* about the subject.
    3. Get command of *still more facts* about the subject.

Yes, that's old stuff. But most of us don't seem to believe it—or, at least, we don't practice it. One rub is that fact getting is to many persons a baffling business. Research, a word highly dramatized during the war, sort of frightens us. Not long ago an ex-Marine came to me (Woolf) in a state of complete confusion. He and his wife had saved about eight thousand dollars, and they were planning on starting a sporting goods store. Both of them liked to hunt and fish and were all-round sports fans; hence they felt they would like the business.

"But there are simply a hundred questions in my mind," the visitor told us despairingly. "And I haven't the foggiest notion how to go about getting the facts I need."

Facts are as free and abundant as the air we breathe. There is no reason why anybody should stumble along in a fog. There are so many sources of information that space will not permit listing them here. But you should know about six we have consulted hundreds of times in thirty years of business practice—at a total cost of not over ten dollars!

Consult your government. One great source is Washington. The United States Government Printing Office issues many thousands of how-to-do-it manuals to help us-to get better results from our undertakings. Alton P. Tisdel, Superintendent of Documents, Washington, D.C., tells us that these manuals "now cover the entire field of human knowledge, and that their importance to us cannot be fully estimated."

Let's suppose, for example, that you want to build something— a workshop, a barn, a storeroom, a trailer camp, a warehouse. The government offers you your choice of 101 manuals on building materials alone, most of them priced at five cents, a few of them at ten to twenty cents.

Or maybe you are planning a truck garden or a farm. Well, the government has ready for you a selection of nearly 2,000 manuals that tell you how to do it. Perhaps, for example, you figure you can make money raising tomatoes. Okay, ask Uncle Sam about it. He offers you thirty-seven manuals on the subject, most of them for a nickel, two or three for a dime, and one of them (an eighty-three-page illustrated book on tomato diseases) for fifteen cents. How can you beat that?

There is practically no branch of commerce and industry not covered by the manuals. Available to you are hundreds of valuable treatises on advertising, selling, cost accounting, credit, purchasing, collections, financing, manufacturing, shipping; the list is endless. No matter what you are mulling over you are pretty sure to get some illuminating information.

The procedure is easy. Just send a postal card to the Superintendent of Documents, United States Government Printing Office, Washington, D.C., state your problem, and back will come a catalog of everything the government has on the subject. A five-cent manual may stop you from making a thousand-dollar mistake.

Consult your trade journals. Nearly two thousand trade journals, covering 170 different classifications of human activity, are published in the United States.

Possibly you don't know much about the trade press. Surprisingly, most people don't. Not long ago, a former lieutenant in the Navy, writing me of his plans to start a small laundry, asked me to suggest a course of helpful reading. I shortly found he had never heard of the fine periodicals devoted to the "how" of running a laundry. The ex-marine and his wife, the sporting goods entrepreneurs already mentioned, also were unaware of the several good business papers in this field.

The latest ideas and discoveries of the scientist, the engineer, the chemist, the inventor, the businessman, the explorer and the experimenter in every field, are promptly reported in the trade journal. A food chemist, after long experiment with ascorbic acid, perfects a way to improve greatly the taste and texture of frozen fish; a scientist finds a way to blend plastics and Fiberglas into a lovely new material, the result of two years of research; an engineer invents a dashboard signal light that warns the motorist that he is driving with his brakes on, and another man works out a method of giving cars a sparkling wash in two minutes; a metallurgist discovers how to treat aluminum to make it nearly 100 per cent safe against burns, stains, and scratches; a grocer thinks up a novel way to keep his vegetables fresh longer; a bookkeeper devises a short cut that reduces his firm's paper work by half. All such discoveries are grist for the trade paper's mill.

Except in rare instances you will not find trade journals on the newsstands, and only a few of them are available in any but the very largest public libraries. The best plan is to take out a yearly subscription, the cost of which will be anywhere from one to four dollars. To find out what business paper you should read, and how you can subscribe to it, talk with a Reader's Adviser at your public library. He has this information or can get it for you.

Consult your public library. Even as a child William Armstrong's absorbing interest was invention. He developed scores of gadgets, but because none of them was sufficiently original his ideas were not salable. After his release from the Army he renewed his experiments, but again they lacked enough novelty to make them marketable. Armstrong found himself not only broke, but in debt.

A friend, hearing of his troubles, begged him to "go to your public library and get the low-down on this invention racket."

Armstrong went. The Reader's Adviser helped him check through patent records on the originality of his ideas. This resulted in his immediate abandonment of half a dozen of his experiments.

The Adviser also gave him books that gave him ideas for inventions. Still other books told him how to patent his inventions and market them. Within a few months he developed two ideas that netted him six thousand dollars.

Millions are missing a good bet in not using their public libraries for research in connection with their ideas and enterprises. Current figures are not at hand, but it has been true in the past that less than 15 per cent of the nation's adults are registered book borrowers. In Chicago, the figure has been as low as 10 per cent; in Philadelphia 5 per cent; in Boston less than 11 per cent; in New Orleans about 7 per cent. These figures refer to *holders* and not necessarily *users* of cards. Moreover, the call is usually for books of fiction and not for books of facts.

There is no better place than your library to reduce your risk by research. It is yours, it is free. Are you using it at all, or as often as you should?

Consult your university. The instructors at your state university, or any college for that matter, can be most helpful. Recently a friend of mine considered going into poultry raising. He called at a Midwestern university and was given two whole hours by the man who heads up the experimental poultry division. He was invited to enroll for the school's extension course in poultry raising, its cost less than the price of a carton of cigarettes. Walking in unannounced on this kindly man, our friend walked away with pockets stuffed with manuals and letters of introduction to several successful poultry farmers who later gave him invaluable advice.

He was talked out of at least five mistakes he could have made!

Another friend of mine had an idea for what he thought might be a highly effective beauty cream. An amateur chemist, he made scores of experiments in his kitchen, but because of some error in his calculations his formula was a failure.

At our suggestion he paid a visit to his state university. The head of the Department of Chemistry listened with interest to the problem, and within an hour put his finger on what he thought was the difficulty. His suggestions for further experiments were carried out, and within two weeks the problem was solved. He might have fumbled along in the dark for years. He didn't—because he got command of the facts.

The modern university is an institution organized for the gathering and study and teaching of facts; its courses embrace every branch of human knowledge; even such practical things as store-keeping, shop management, and bee culture. Many universities offer extension courses that bring their know-how at very slight cost, right into your home.

Consult your Chamber of Commerce. Four years ago a Chicago man moved, because of poor health, to a small western high-altitude city. Only forty, and hoping he had a long time to live, it was clear that his savings, about fifteen thousand dollars, would not support him for long.

For years an amateur painter and student of the arts, it was his plan to establish a combination gift shop and art gallery in his adopted city. He figured that his savings, plus a loan of five thousand dollars, would be enough to get the business going.

One day, before he was in very deep, he paid a courtesy call on his local Chamber of Commerce. He went in for a minute, stayed more than an hour, came out completely unsold on the enterprise he had been planning. The Chamber of Commerce manager was against it. There were already too many art-and-gift shops in the town; two shops within the last year had closed their doors; the proposed side-street location of the contemplated shop was bad, and no good ones were available in the desirable shopping areas.

The community, declared the Chamber of Commerce man, was a natural for a dairy farm. There were not nearly enough dairy farms to supply the county, and 45 per cent of the city's milk was shipped in from as far away as three hundred miles. The market was a good one.

The Chicago man had made his home on a farm when he lived in Illinois and for years had raised dairy cows as a hobby. He accepted the suggestion with alacrity and immediately began reducing his risk with research. That was four years ago. Today he is a dairy farmer in most comfortable circumstances; and, what's more, thanks to his outdoor life, his former ill health is only a memory.

Talk with the manager of your local Chamber of Commerce before plunging into a venture of your own. You'll find he knows your town or city, statistically speaking, as intimately as you know the back of your hand. It is his business to encourage the launching of healthy businesses in his community and to discourage poor risks.

Consult your banker. The old notion of the banker as an unsmiling, steely-eyed penny pincher is out of date. The modern banker has a genuine, if selfish, interest in encouraging new enterprises in his community; he knows that a prosperous, growing community means a prosperous, growing bank. He wants you to be successful.

Talk over your idea with your banker. His advice may help you avoid making costly mistakes. One man I know, the owner of a print shop, eager to get ahead fast, went to his banker with an ambitious plan for expansion. He wanted to borrow twenty thousand dollars to finance additional presses and an added wing to his building.

The banker sat down with the printer and analyzed in detail the financial possibilities of such a program. He had statistics on the annual dollar volume of printing in the town, and he had private information that the printer's biggest customer, a mail-order house, was planning to move its offices to another state.

He helped the printer figure his probable future sales and cost of doing business under the proposed enlarged set-up, including the cost of financing the loan, and it soon was apparent that the scheme was hazardous. The banker recommended an expansion program not to exceed five thousand dollars in cost, a suggestion the printer agreed to. Subsequent events over the next two years demonstrated the soundness of the banker's advice. The printer would undoubtedly have gone under if he had gone through with his twenty-thousand-dollar expansion dream.

You will find your banker always glad to sit down with you and talk over your plans, even if your enterprise is nothing more ambitious than a little roadside restaurant.

Successful businessmen of wide experience take a long, hard look before they leap. The makers of a new breakfast cereal specialty held off launching the product for three years while they sought command of *facts*, *more facts*, and *still more facts*. When, finally, the facts looked good, they made one more research move. They packaged only eight thousand cartons of their product and put it on sale for three months in forty stores. Then and only then, after it was certain that the public liked the item, were they ready to introduce it nationally.

Use your imagination all the time. Make it work for you. Never let it rest. But temper your decisions with information. Get facts, facts, facts about anything before you act. If you put imagination on your team, and then make information a teammate of imagination, you can't lose. This is a *fact*. It is a fact proved by hundreds of thousands of successful, happy lives every year.

Why can't you also prove it in yours?

One night last week I (Woolf) made $500 while I slept.

It happened this way: A certain advertiser of a food product had commissioned me to create a slogan for him. For days I struggled with the problem, but the deathless phrase wouldn't come. I decided to quit trying.

Then I awoke last Wednesday morning after a night of peaceful slumber, and there were the magic words spelled out in neon on the ceiling of my room.

My unconscious mind had done the trick. No doubt you have had a like experience. Inspiration has come to you while you were fishing, or playing bridge or reading a whodunit. Grant Wood, famous "painter of the soil," once said that "all good ideas I ever had came to me while I was milking." When Sir Walter Scott found himself completely baffled, he turned his mind to something else, sure that the idea would come. "I shall have it at 7 o'clock tomorrow morning," he'd say.

Do you have any control over your unconscious mind? Can you prod it into doing a bigger job for you? The answer, I think, is "yes" to both questions, and most psychologists would, I believe, back me up. For many years I did creative work in a large advertising agency, one of the most demanding of "idea businesses." I found that three things must be done:

Number One: *I must soak up the facts.*

I cannot recall ever producing a good idea—either consciously or in my sleep—until I had done hours or days of thorough study.

"Inspiration," Alfred Tennyson once declared, "comes after effort."

Hermann von Heimholtz, the great German physicist, once declared that "after investigating a problem in all directions," happy ideas came to him "without effort, like an inspiration." The wife of Maeterlinck reported that he never expected inspiration until after he had first saturated his mind with facts. "I can testify," she asserted, "that his subconscious played a formidable role."

Number Two: *I must forget the whole thing.*

I once sat at my desk for 24 hours trying to think up an idea for an automobile tire. That was silly, and now I know better. When inspiration eludes you after a fair amount of mental effort, put away your notes and go out to a movie. Think back. Have you ever forced an idea out of a tired brain by grim "concentration" over a prolonged period?

Listen to Paul Gallico. He comments on this very thing in his book Confessions of a Story Writer. He had half an idea for a yarn. But the plot "simply wouldn't jell," Gallico tells us. Did he sit at his desk for 24 hours and try to sweat it out? Not he! He wisely decided to forget the whole thing. Then a year later, during a symphony concert he was attending at Carnegie Hall, he relates that "the solution suddenly popped up from nowhere and the story simply rolled forth. I wrote out the ideas on the margin of the program and finished the piece within a week."

Hector Berlioz, the French composer, once tried to write a song with chorus for *Cinq Mai*, of Beranger, but he was utterly stumped by a difficult refrain. So he shoved the problem aside into some inner compartment of his mind.

Two years later, on rising from a dive in the Tiber, Berlioz found himself humming the wanted musical phrase.

Igo Etrich was not hunched over a drawing board when he invented the Taube flying machine. He had tried that with no luck. Later, vacationing in India and bent on enjoying himself, he happened to notice that the seed of an Indian vine, the zancnia, floated through the air with perfect grace and balance. Up from his unconscious emerged his forgotten problem, and at once he had his idea for his famous wing principle.

Number Three: *I must brief my mind at bedtime.*

A noted editor once told me that at bedtime, just before he turns out his light, he reads over the notes he has made on some problem that perplexes him. I have tried his system and it works.

Alexander Graham Bell did a lot of his thinking while he slept. "I make it a point," he once said, "to bring together all the facts regarding a problem before I retire." Often a problem that troubled Bell the night before was found to be solved perfectly the next morning.

Halftone printing was invented by a man in his slumber. Frederic Eugene Ives testified that while operating his photostereotype process in Ithaca, New York, he studied the problem of the halftone process. He went to bed one night, his mind briefed on the problem as he fell asleep, and awoke in the morning to see before his eyes, apparently projected on the ceiling, the completely worked-out process and equipment in operation.

So don't knock yourself out by trying to force your imagination. It can't be forced. Relax, give it a chance—and how it will deliver!

COACHWHIP PUBLICATIONS

COACHWHIPBOOKS.COM

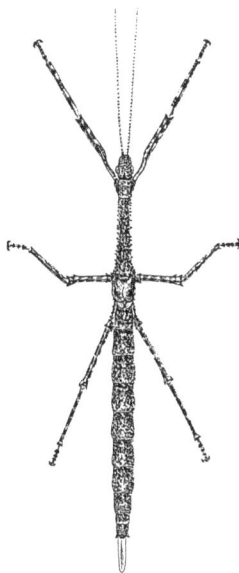

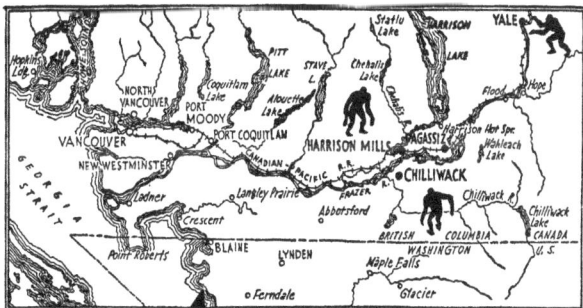

www.ingramcontent.com/pod-product-compliance
Lightning Source LLC
Chambersburg PA
CBHW030011290326

41934CB00005B/295